T0065215

And God saw everything that He had made was perfect. The evening and the morning were the sixth day. God blessed the seventh day; and sanctified it: because in the seventh day, He rested from all His work which He created.

Power in God's Word

"I Change Not"

(Malachi 3:6)

Therefore, your sons and daughters shall not perish.

DAVID SHAWN MOSBY

"I CHANGE NOT"
POWER IN GOD'S WORD

iUniverse books may be ordered through booksellers or by contacting:

iUniverse
1663 Liberty Drive
Bloomington, IN 47403
www.iuniverse.com
844-349-9409

Scripture quotations from the Holy Bible, King James Version (Authorized Version). First published in 1611. Quoted from the KJV Classic Reference Bible.

Unless otherwise indicated, all scripture quotations are from The Holy Bible, English Standard Version® (ESV®). Copyright ©2001 by Crossway Bibles, a division of Good News Publishers. Used by permission. All rights reserved.

Scripture quotations marked NIV are taken from the Holy Bible, New International Version®. NIV®. Copyright © 1973, 1978, 1984 by International Bible Society. Used by permission of Zondervan. All rights reserved. [Biblica]

ISBN: 978-1-6632-1431-7 (sc)
ISBN: 978-1-6632-1432-4 (e)

Library of Congress Control Number: 2020924063

Print information available on the last page.

iUniverse rev. date: 12/16/2020

Table of Contents

Introduction...vii

Chapter 1: Truth... 1

Chapter 2: Prophets... 14

Chapter 3: A Time for Silence 37

Chapter 4: The Period of Silence..59

Chapter 5: Protection 73

Chapter 6: The Second Adam... 110

Chapter 7: Soft-Spoken Whisper...148

Chapter 8: Power by Faith in Love 174

Introduction

It's amazing how God uses history to work out His purpose. There was a time that may be called "the silence of God," and even today it seems at times that God is silent. But is God quiet, or are we not listening?

I remember my grandmother taking me to church when I was about five years old. I saw the rejoicing and praising, heard the testimonies, and then listened to the preaching, and it was all uplifting to my grandmother. I tried to figure out what was happening to the people to make them do and say what they did. As I got older and the Word of God began speaking into my life through the voices of my parents, grandparents, relatives, teachers, and friends. I began to pay attention to what was happening around me.

At eight years old, I sassed my mother's girlfriend and ran so the friend couldn't get to me. She told me that she was not going to run after me, but that God would fix things so that I'd get chastised. I thumbed my nose at her. Much later, however, my mother, her girlfriend, my older brother, and I went fishing at a local park. My brother and I left my mother to get a drink of water, and a group of older boys surrounded us at the water fountain. My brother told me to drink first, but then while he was drinking, the boys picked me up by my arms and legs, swung me back and forth three times, and laughed as they hurled my body into the lake. I wasn't a great swimmer, but I treaded water until the boys left. While I was in the water, I remembered sassing my mother's girlfriend and then hearing her say, as I ran away, "God will fix it."

Later in life, I walked into my mother's church with my family. The ushers at the door greeted me with dignity, and they asked if I was a minister and what church I pastored. I told them I was not a pastor but a visitor on behalf of my mother. The church members treated me with dignity. But as I grew older, I was learning to walk with Christ while my prayer change things. I got a new biblical language through study. I listened to people's prayers and watched how God worked in their lives and changed them. But what was profound was the way the people were so gracious when they thanked and praised God.

As a law enforcement officer, I nearly lost my life early one morning. A preacher and his deacon were showing me how a burglar got into their church through a basement window. As we were walking down a long hall, we approached a door through which the three of us would not fit at the same time. I stepped back, and the preacher and deacon walked through the door side by side. On the other side of the door, a man with a gun suddenly stepped out with his arm raised. I was behind the preacher and the deacon, centered between them, and the gun was pointed directly at my face. The man was looking at me through holes cut into the leg of a pair of pants. Startled at seeing a policeman, he began pulling the trigger and the gun's cylinder began to turn. I saw the bullets rotating upward toward the barrel. The preacher grabbed the cylinder of the gun before it fired, and the deacon pinned the man against the wall. My entire life had flashed before my eyes while that gun was pointed at me.

After replaying the incident over and over in my mind, I mentally quit the police department. I got up day after day, got dressed, and made the journey to the police station to work, but my heart was not in the service to the public. I went to work still replaying that incident in my head, seeing the hood over that man's head with the eye holes cut out. His eyes had been cold and calculating, revealing no remorse as he was pulling the trigger. Then I could realize my prayers, sincere and genuinely thankful to God.

Now, remembering going to church with my grandmother, hearing those testimonies, the praises, and the preached Word of God were nuggets towards my spiritual life. All that resonates today in my heart. The worship services, Holy Communion, testifying, and preaching to everybody is the "will" of God. Later in life, early one morning in the breeze blowing off Lake Providence in Louisiana, I heard the voice of God say within my heart, "Learn of Me and teach."

Shortly after that, I acknowledged my ministry. I attended ministry studies under Reverend Dr. Rodney Howlett Sr. in Alorton, Illinois, and received a Certificate of Ordination and a Certificate of Achievement. Later I received a Certificate of License under the direction of Reverend Dr. Ercyle Davis in St. Louis, Missouri. I served the Lord under the command of Pastor Davis, ministering to everybody; men, women, children; those who were made whole by the gospel of Christ, the spiritually broken and the mentally and physically sick, those saved and the unsaved.

In my studies, I got an understanding. I chose to preach the

Word of God as the Holy Spirit illustrates to me through His teaching. My prayer to God is for His Word to teach me the more profound things of the Word, so that I may teach others the Truth. My journey through life has been remarkable, but not without a manifested profound belief in God through study and counseling by the Holy Spirit. God did not call me to pastor a congregation in a building, but to minister to all people, planting seeds that one day He'll bring to fruition.

For more than two thousand years, there haven't been any inspired writers to add to the biblical writings from God. Looking back, even during those four hundred silent years between the Old and New Testaments, the inspired record, we realize that God has already said all that needed to be told through the Old Testament, and then He revealed what He said in the New Testament. God's purpose has not ended or changed. He's working purposefully and fully today, just as He did yesterday. The world had come to a place of hopelessness during the Old Testament period, and the promise of hope was on the table but not fully consummated. Today that hope is still on the table, but are there more devout laborers?

The One who could fulfill all our hopes came into the world after the total eradication of some people, and thus new generations began without plausible evidence of God. They had only writings and stories on which to base their beliefs, following the Old Testament. And as a result of having only written documents and word-of-mouth knowledge, the later generations leading up to the New Testament period, after the four hundred years of silence, based their expectations and hope on Jesus.

Today despair is again spreading widely across the earth, not as in the Old Testament era, but because of the lackadaisical beliefs of spiritually uninformed people. Hopelessness is rampant everywhere, and God is moving to fulfill the prophetic words concerning the nature and divinity of His Son. God's kingdom is as He said it is, but do we have to die to experience His kingdom? What must we do to obtain favor and experience kingdom living while we are alive? Is there a kingdom of God, both now and after death? Was Jesus real, and is He coming back? Who knows? Does anybody know?

What has God done throughout history? He has ordained people, and He's still ordaining. He is still managing as He's always done. As we approach the end of our lifetime, the Lord has not changed His commitment to His purpose. People must repent and become obedient to the will of God, learning to love one another as God has loved us all.

Was there silence between the Old and New Testament periods, or did the people not hear God?

There were four hundred years of silence between the times of the Old and New Testaments during which God did not speak to the people. The four hundred years of silence began when the Old Testament era ended with a warning concerning a savior, a Messiah, whom the people would seek for atonement for their sin. The Messiah, the One whom God spoke of for the atonement for the people, would create the pathway for the righteous to come back to God. Sin in the garden of Eden caused God to implement the law—that is, guidelines for the people to follow. God implemented a structured system of commands and promises regulating human affairs, which mandated God's way of life.

But the people conformed to their fleshly desires rather than being thankful for God's grace and mercies. Many of them acknowledged God but didn't believe in Him. Some thought of men as earthly gods, and others hailed celestial gods for certain things such as crops, rain, wind, fertility, and so on. Some people could not keep the law because their human nature desired to sin. Others did not support the law; their beliefs became tainted toward the goodwill of others that forced them against honoring the law. Failing to observe God's law resulted in physical hardships, confinement, and ultimately death. It was tough to manage the gift of life because of the struggle of balancing it with the law.

Some people hoped for "the One" to save them and bring order to their land, and so they waited. Many waited and succumbed to death, and their bodies were disposed of without hope of the One to save them.

All bodies once lived in the heavens, but not everyone will rest eternally in the sky. The earthly body is ideally suited to life on earth, whereas the heavenly body is made honorable after the physical. Nevertheless, there is a vast difference between the two groups. The celestial body is calm and in control of its emotions, not feeling or showing anger or fear, but free from agitation.

An earthly body that lived separate from God shall be eternally separated from God. Since God is light and the absence of God is darkness, then hell must be more than just a mental state of mind, and it must be a place of utter darkness. Hell must be any place where God is absent, a place of everlasting torment, the home of Satan. The absence of God is the absence of light, and the weeping will be eternal tears of regret for not having believed in Jesus.

The earthly body, an aggregation of matter constituting a whole, is composed of elements including hydrogen, oxygen, carbon, calcium, and phosphorus. The physical body is composed of many distinct parts, such as a nervous system of neurons that form the nerves and ganglia, which in turn create a brain and related structures. The brain is the organ of thought, emotion, memory, and sensory functions serving vision, hearing, taste, touch, smell, and the ability to form a judgment. Some parts can operate independently of each other, and others depend on one another.

Like the universe, the distinct parts of the body constitute a unit of integrated characteristics. And like the universe, all types of people are included and participate in the family. People don't need anyone else to survive, and our existence is not dependent upon that of anyone else. But our existence is influenced by another whose trust, energy, knowledge, finances, touch, smell, emotions, and so on shape our personality.

Man has developed a system of accountability in which we measure someone by how another person treats them, and we reciprocate with the same degree of affection. For this reason, we've come to be judgmental and form our own opinions based on how our psyche is influenced by what others say or what we've observed, and then we act out. Because forgiveness carries no weight once we've judged a person, relationships become strained based on the trials and errors of others. Then forgiveness is virtually mandated by man's thoughts and feelings and predicated on man's will. The detriment to unforgiveness, whereby we err, is on the side of Satan and not Christ. The error is that we separate ourselves from God's sure foundation because we don't know Him. We choose unforgiveness over forgiveness, which is how people become separated from God.

The splendor of heavenly bodies is one thing, and the wonder of earthly bodies is another. We are a spirit with a soul that lives in a human being. It is our immaterial force within our human nature that gives our bodies life, energy, and power, and our immortal souls will live forever, long after our earthly bodies are dead and buried. The immaterial intelligent attitude is the part that connects to God and covers matters such as faith, trust, and worship. The firmness then is asserted as the innermost part of our being. It is enveloped by our soul, which, in turn, is encompassed by our body. Our whole spirit, soul, and body must be kept blameless for the coming of the One, our Lord and Savior, the Messiah.

Approximately four hundred years passed in which God didn't speak to man, according to the Bible. Four hundred years is how much time passed, but God lives in eternity. Four hundred years might be a long time for man, but it may have seemed like only a few hours to God! Eternity is our destiny as we travel through time, and God has given us a choice for our final resting place, either the kingdom of God with Him or hell with Satan.

The One, the Messiah, is not to be misunderstood as God's purpose for the earth. Nevertheless, this foundation, God's plan for the Messiah, will ensure that the Lord knows who is His. Everyone who names Christ as their Savior will depart from Satan, purge themselves from iniquity, and become vessels of honor, and meet God's use prepared for every good work.

CHAPTER 1

Truth

> Truth is what is spoken by God;
> He cannot lie for He is God,
> What He says,
> He will bring to pass.

THE BIBLE OPENS WITH; IN the beginning God created the Heaven and the Earth. God, who was present before the beginning of time, created heaven and earth. The Bible tells us the world was without form, void, in an ample space, and it was absent of all things. The surrounding area was dark, and the Spirit of God moved upon the face of the waters. We are at the origin of all things, and there's nothing in ancient books that contradicts the Bible's story of these events. God divided the light from the darkness, called the light good, and then established the first day. Beyond the first day, man developed weeks, months, and years implementing systems to track time according to his knowledge, not God's.

God formed the sun, moon, and stars. The closest to the earth is the moon, and the farthest planet is unknown to humanity because you don't know what you don't know. From the creation of time to a short time ago, it was a gigantic feat for man to get to the moon. Man didn't think it was possible to get there, but today moon travel is feasible. Stars are so distant that man still has not developed the technology to get to even the closest one. And is the conquest of the sun practical? Maybe someday. Man began focusing on the sun's attributes, whereas God's focus is on the Son's facts.

God said, "Let us make man in our image and after our likeness. And let them have dominion over the fish, the fowl, the cattle, and all the earth. Let man also have dominion over every creeping thing that creeps upon the earth." God speaks of Himself in the plural form: "Let us …" Who is God? This statement is an indication that God is one God with multiple persons, meaning He's a triune God—Father, Son, and Holy Spirit, three persons in one God!

The Bible tells us the Spirit of God moved upon the face of the waters, and God said, Let there be light, and there was light. Now the Spirit of God is in the earth realm, and the light of God is within the earth's sphere. God spoke light into the earth's field. The record goes on with God speaking things into existence and numbering the days of creation one through six.

Today, a day is the length of time it takes the earth to make a complete revolution, so that the entire planet experiences both light and dark. God is Spirit and moved across the deep, so the Spirit could have been anywhere on the globe or covering the entire planet. So neither the earth's revolutions nor the positioning of the sun could have mattered. However, the significance of the voice of God is important.

Many of us accept the words "God created the heaven" without thought of the entity. Especially in our youth, we have heard the word *heaven*, but we have no conscious idea of the particular conditions attributed to a heaven-bound journey. Life is about enjoying personal freedom and not being subject to the control of another's dominion. We can't fathom a mandate structured by God under truth, but we will be judged by our actions according to that truth. As we age, we become more familiar with the idea of heaven. We become aware of mystical events that have no logical explanations, and we begin accepting and believing consciously the things we've heard.

The earth is a cruel teacher, and lessons are either caught by observation or bought through disobedience. Nevertheless, the voice of the earth will speak. In most scenarios dealing with the planet, a thought process perceives the decision, and our actions are direct responses to an outcome that is good, threatening, or indifferent. We come to know things about the earth through the consequences of our actions. We should learn from the experiences and activities of ourselves and others. We ought to consider the results as conclusively factual, for the evidence points toward causes and effects being real. We're the processors of the knowledge that the actions manufacture. Our decisions are derived from the results as the activities pertain to us, whether good or bad. The results are what they are, and this we know. On the other hand, there seems to be a mystical place without facts to substantiate another existence. The dilemma becomes weighing our decisions, actions, and results concerning doing something against being bound to heaven, the unsubstantiated mystical place.

Heaven, a place of grandeur, appeals to the mind. We've all heard remarkable stories of this wonderful place and seen beautiful pictures depicting heaven. The beautiful, impressive place fills us with amazement and eases the mind into a tranquil state. In this mystical place, a person finds rest and enjoyment, becomes calm and free of stress, experiences tranquility, and enters into oneness with God.

The truth is that God created heaven and earth. We know the earth exists, so why not believe in heaven? One reason may be that nobody has confirmed the existence of heaven. We cannot comprehend by sense or imagination what heaven is or is not. I suppose that to learn the real reason He said there is a heaven, we will have to ask our Creator, God.

But I do know that God, through His Word, tells us to keep heaven in our sight and the earth under our feet. That same Spirit that moved across the deep is leading us to a glorious place of rest, and we are to have lofty ideas about heaven, a place we're not sure exists. Is this a tall order? Yes, it is.

Can we do it? Yes, but not by ourselves, since God's enemy is on earth, warring with our flesh. The enemy of God is a spirit that influences our flesh with lust and worldly things. This spirit uses trickery and falsehoods—delusion, error, fallacy, falsity, hallucination, illusion, misbelief, misconception, myth, old wives' tales, and untruths—to disrupt our stability and composure on our life's journey. God's enemy is powerless to confront God directly, so he obstructs us from the progress of God's plan for us.

The voice of God is always present within the earth realm. God has given His creation—man—free will to express his/her desires, choices, willingness, and consent, but we can choose to exercise our expression in negative ways. Choosing a godly understanding of God and to express ourselves for our self-worth towards God is God's right way of going about life. The distribution of our desires account for our explanations throughout life and is attributed to godliness or our refusals to express God's commands, exhortations, or injunctions. Man's unwillingness to choose God's plan for himself is a detriment to humanity.

Those who choose to hear the voice of God over the enemy's spirit select the quality of being blessed, which is entirely delightful in a pleasant and uniquely divine nature. The choice of hearing God's voice involves not only hearing but also obeying. What we hear does not always make sense or mean the way is straight. We may encounter bumps, lumps, and even death, but the outcome is what is important to God. Giving up life in the earthly realm is sometimes part of reaching a future outlined by God.

Son and Sun

The Son, a part of the triune personality of God, is significant to the Spirit that moved across the deep, because He was an example of the truth in the Bible. The Son of God took on flesh and blood, and then He walked the earth as a man, teaching with words and by example about God. The character of the Son, Jesus, was humble enough to destroy the will of the enemy by becoming the Word of God on earth and establishing God's Word through promises.

God's enemy is competent in the management of practical affairs and manufactured schemes used against God's people through their independence and prestige. He interjected selfishness and human individuality into freedom and used them as weapons of warfare against man. God's enemy is a spirit, and his weapons are spiritual, but man is carnal and cannot fight nature in spiritual warfare with carnal weapons.

God's Son, Lord Jesus, delivered God's spiritual power into the earthly realm with the Word of God through the knowledge of the Father. The Word of God is man's spiritual weapon against the enemy. Defeating the enemy's mental deployment makes room for changes that benefit the will of God in guiding humanity toward heaven. Lord Jesus, the Messiah, our hope, converts creation through acknowledging love and trusting God, receiving Him and His promises through obedience, and thus restoring lives for eternal life in heaven.

The sun provides life through light, warmth, and energy. Sunlight makes it possible for us to see, and sight arouses our sensations and stimulates strong feelings that direct physiological and behavioral changes in our bodies. Hummingbirds flap their wings so fast that we can't see them, although we know the wings are there, enabling the bird to remain still while extracting nectar from flowers. We can see the bird, but not its wings, just like we can see the sun, but not the energy it's providing the flower to manufacture the nectar. Nor can we know the power given the plant to grow, but we see the bird fly and drink the nectar, and the plant survives. These things we know because we witness the effects of the sun's energy.

The effects of the Son are similar to the effects of the sun in the sky. However, because the Son is part of the Godhead, He is superior and praiseworthy. The Son has an exceptional ability to make each of us into unique individuals, though with like-minded characteristics. Created with perishable bodies, humans are given spiritual qualities and a set of innate values that need development. We are born equipped with some merits, but other characteristics are developed or acquired through experience. The method by which we obtain knowledge can have a measurable and significant role in our journey toward our destination. The hummingbird has wings that allow it to feed, and although we don't see how it maintains stillness in flight, we know it eats.

Based upon belief, the Son builds our most holy faith predicated on the notion that He is who He says He is, and that belief is in one Lord, one faith, and one baptism in the Father. Like the hummingbird, which stops in midair to feed, moving from one flower to another, our understanding is mystifying but golden, so get all the knowledge you can get. Remember, God made the hummingbird too.

There is one Lord, one baptism, and one faith. One Lord is the object of our faith, and both Jews and Gentiles believe in that Lord. One baptism means that everyone is baptized into the one Lord upon profession of faith. Being faithful means believing without seeing. The hummingbird's wings move too fast for the naked eye to see, but they are there. Faith believes without seeing.

God created heaven and earth. We see earth, but where is heaven? Heaven is a place where our spirits go after we transition from natural life through death to eternal life. Nobody can explain heaven in a way that can be truly understood, so there's a bit of skepticism and mystery about it, just as there is skepticism and mystery about the wings of a hummingbird in flight. If you slowed down a video of a hummingbird in flight, you could see how the bird uses its wings to sustain flight and maneuver. The mystery of a hummingbird's abilities in flight is learned, and now we can understand how it flies, stops, and moves from one plant to another. So what was unlearned is now understood. Similarly, the mystery of heaven is not a mystery but is unlearned.

Yes, God created heaven by speaking it into existence. But the place of bliss is not easily described or made known by man because we imagine it rather than studying it. To discover where heaven is, we must look further into the record of God creating heaven and earth.

God is Spirit, so we refer to a vast body of darkness where God is. After He spoke heaven and earth into existence, the earth and sky were in disarray as He moved across the deep space. God is a God of order and decency, so He walked across the face of the earth surveying and determining sizes, shapes, and boundaries on this barren, lifeless, desolate landscape. God designed places and conditions for utmost happiness. Heaven and earth were outfitted to be pleasant and enjoyable places where complete satisfaction and autonomy could be experienced.

The word *firmament* is responsible for the mystery about heaven. Researchers have studied this word and come up with results based on the theory of the hummingbird. Did God create the hummingbird itself, or did He design a world in which the bird came to exist? Remember, nobody was here to influence God or offer suggestions as He engaged in creating the world. Researchers have studied religious systems based on the seeking of self-knowledge and spiritual fulfillment through graded courses of study and training. Man's understanding is based on facts and logic that can be studied and explained rationally.

In the Bible, God asked a prophet where was he when God laid the foundations of the earth? Then God asked if the prophet had an understanding? The prophet had no answer for this line of questioning. God asked him a fundamental question that denotes the distinction between God's wisdom and man's understanding, as related to the creation of humanity and man's knowledge of nature.

Scholars attempt to answer the question of what is meant by the mystical word *firmament*. Even a knowledgeable audience may be unfamiliar with the meaning of *firmament*. In one translation of the Bible, *firmament* is used to describe a vast, insubstantial expanse that stretches and extends. The Bible depicts the firmament as a significant arching expansion of space above our heads. In the firmament, a mass of air surrounds the earth with clouds above the ground. Stars appear to be placed in the firmament, where the planets lack substance and mass. What we see are the gaseous states of the celestial bodies known as planets.

We now know that expanse as *space*, where God said to let there be a firmament amid the waters, dividing the waters from the waters. Then God made the firmament and divided the waters under the firmament from the waters above the firmament, and it was so. And God called the firmament heaven.

The language of scripture is not scientific, but it is accessible. We read of the sun rising and setting, and it is plain through scripture that the firmament denoted solidity as well as expansion.

The firmament formed a division between the waters above and the waters below, denoting space. Scripture suggests the existence of an upper reservoir, and it supports the idea that heavenly bodies have windows and doors through which the rain and snow might descend.

The Bible says that God spoke the firmament into existence, and within the firmament, everything that God created was created for a purpose.

On the second day, God made the firmament, the sky, heaven, a vast expanse. The waters were divided under and above the firmament that God called heaven. Also, on the second day, the firmament divided the waters on earth. The dry land was called earth, and the ground is the surface in heaven.

On the third day, the firmament, heaven, was illuminated by the light dividing the day from the night. The view is to be signs for seasons, days, and years, and the sun to rule the day over the night.

Creation came out of nothing, and it's clear that God is the Creator, but how did He create this world? He gives the answer to those of us who believe that He is God.

As the Spirit moved across the deep emptiness of space, nothing had been created. During creation, God established order. The Spirit put the waters, land, stars, sun, and moon in their respective places and then made earth accountable for the separation between the seasons and day and night. Then, so that life could thrive, the Spirit placed conditions on food chains to assure the survival of everything that He had created. Then God rested.

God gave purpose to His creation of humanity. Humanity consisted of male and female, and their abilities, subjectivity, and emotions contributed to the achievement of His goal. Humanity acquired traits such as taste, dignity, quality, politeness, morality, honest behavior, respectful attitudes toward others—and above all, worship and obedience to God. These are the essential spiritual character traits of God Himself.

The earth was placed within heaven and given all the heavenly qualities. God put man, His creation, into the garden of Eden, which contained all that man needed to survive. The garden included various types of vegetation, some of which were good for food. God told man to dress the garden but not to eat the fruit from the tree in the middle of the garden. This one tree was forbidden. Man could eat any other fruit that was fit to eat, but if he ate the fruit from the tree in the middle of the garden, he would definitely die. The forbidden tree was the Tree of Knowledge of Good and Evil. If man listened to God and obeyed God's commandment, he would live forever. Man did not need knowledge of good and evil, because he had God as the source for holy living and life on earth.

God created for the man a partner, a woman, but for His purpose. Her job was to nurture, support, have children, and be a companion. The serpent performed an underhanded act of deception to win over God, taking advantage of the woman's sense of pleasure. Convinced that the forbidden fruit was good to eat, she ate some, and her attributes of being nurturing and strengthening her companionship became active. Her male companion watched her eat the fruit, and when she gave it to him, he ate some too. This act was in direct disobedience of the commandment given to him by God. This act changed God's perspective about creation having access to the Tree of Life and free will to live forever in sin. The consequence for disobedience was death. The man and his companion were separated from the Tree of Life and turned out into the world.

Did the Spirit stop leading? No, God met men and women right where they were in their sin, but they did not, could not, and would not hear Him. Some could not recognize the voice of God, and others attributed their successes to pagan gods, sorcery, and idolizing men and women above God.

Earth was in a heavenly place, but it was becoming a place of hell. Men and women developed behaviors contrary to holiness. People established ruling classes and ruled over the lower classes while considering themselves to be proper and acceptable rulers. They developed habits of behavior that seemed ethical to some but were harmful to others. They prescribed manners of behavior that tainted good morals and declared people to be subject to one or the other. The heavens became a celestial realm, and earth became a dwelling place for those who would die. The idea of eternal life, whether in hell or heaven, dissipated, and only a handful of people remained dedicated followers of the living God.

The heavens do declare the glory of God and proclaim His wisdom, power, and goodness, which all ungodly men and women are without—and they're without excuse. We speak of ourselves as the work of God's hands, for we must have a Creator who is eternal, infinitely wise, all-powerful, and competent, who will show us a positive direction in the way of duty. God provides the sure fountain for living comforts and lasting hopes—one Lord, one faith, and one baptism in the Lord. The statutes of the Lord are right, just as they should be, and because they are correct, they cause the heart to rejoice. The commandments of the Lord are pure, holy, just, and reasonable, and by them, we discover our need of a Savior and learn how to enhance the appearance of His gospel. The Holy Spirit uses the gospels to enlighten our eyes, and they bring us to see our sin and misery and then direct us in the way of duty.

What we see about heaven and earth we have learned through the power of our great Creator by His Word, the truth. Let us take our places as men and women of God, remembering our heavenly duty as Christians. Let us always keep heaven in our eye and the earth under our feet, while striving for the personality of our Lord.

David, a Bible character who is responsible for the book of Psalms, was known as a man after God's heart. He was a worshipper, a warrior, and a worker, but he was human also. His humanity exceeded his call to worship, going beyond the ethics of war to accomplish his human desires, which were in conflict with his devotion to God. But he never forgot his love for God and continuously approached Him, sincerely confessing his sins and asking for forgiveness. God had consistently demonstrated His power on behalf of David, to accomplish His purpose through David. God forgave David's crime, though he had to accept the consequences, but he realized there was no greater love than that of God. David talked and prayed to God with great adoration as if God were a person. He believed that God heard him, and he trusted God. God did save David and deliver him out of all his unrighteousness. God delivered David out of all the personal experiences that he got himself into. God convinced David that He was real, and if we commit our ways unto the Lord and trust in Him, He shall deliver us. We can choose life by accepting Jesus, taking the Word of God as our guide, and emulating the character of Jesus through belief. With belief comes trust and relying on the truthfulness in the Word by the Holy Spirit, while becoming devoted to God as our Father in our earthly bodies on earth as it is in heaven by faith.

CHAPTER 2

Prophets

Men and women divinely
inspired by God as
messengers ordained
and gifted spiritually
with moral insight to
foretell events according to
doctrine.

IMAGINE WALKING DOWN A STREET and hearing a voice
that seems to be coming out of a bush! That probably would scare

us almost to death or cause us to do something irrational and detrimental to ourselves. Startled, we'd perhaps try to put distance between ourselves and the source of the voice. We'd most likely run until we found someone and told them about the mysterious voice, but they would seriously think that we didn't have good sense. I suspect they'd think, *If this is not a joke, either you or I should be committed to a psychiatric hospital for treatment.* Fear of the unknown, especially involving things unearthly or supernatural, causes us to do things that depart from acceptable standards of normality.

The sound of a voice inexplicably coming from a bush would leave us baffled and mentally disturbed. In an attempt at self-preservation, the body reacts in ways that could be mentally or physically harmful, thus justifying being committed to a psychiatric hospital for care. Imagine hearing a voice that seems to come from nowhere talking to you! What would you do? Would you be afraid?

The Spirit of God had conversations with people throughout the historical period covered by the Bible, but one man, Moses, stands out, even though he was not the first. The Spirit of God spoke to His first human creation, Adam, in the garden of Eden, giving him the commandment about how to live eternally and instructing him on the provision by which to sustain himself. Adam was warned about the disastrous consequence of not adhering to the commandment, but his surroundings offset his natural sense of caution.

The book of Revelation records the story of a war that took place in heaven between Archangel Michael and the beautiful angel Satan. The archangel Michael and his angels fought against the dragon, the devil, Satan, and his imps, and Michael won. The war occurred because Satan wanted to rise above God, but there is no place above God. The defeated devil and his demons were cast out of the heavenly realm and into the earthly realm.

Let it be known that Satan has many names—the devil, the serpent—and that he's an enemy of God who deceives the people of God and the entire world. As the serpent, he beguiled Eve emotionally with a twisted analogy about God's Word. Yes, Adam and Eve were created in the image of God, they ate the forbidden fruit, and their eyes were opened to the difference between good and evil. Because they had some of the qualities of God, they had no reason to know about good and evil. If they had kept their minds on God, He would have kept them in perfect peace.

Eve failed to recognize the serpent's scheme, and she thought the forbidden tree was pleasant to the eye and good for food. She also came to believe that the tree could make them wise, so she ate the fruit and gave some to Adam. The reason why Adam disobeyed God is unknown, but he ate the fruit too. Because of the serpent's hatred for God, whom he cannot defeat, God's creation fell from grace through disobedience. Probably Eve's influence, coupled with the twisted knowledge from Satan, influenced Adam to disobey God's commandment. Satan's goal was not to destroy God, but to destroy His creation, man.

God ended His work of creation—heaven, earth, and all the hosts—and rested on the seventh day. Along with the commandment to Adam about how to live eternally came the consequences for not adhering to the commandment—that man will surely die. Once the commandment was broken, Adam and Eve were driven out of the garden and away from the Tree of Life. They began bearing children, who bore children for generations to come.

God established Adam with leadership, and everybody who

came after him was to follow God as mandated through Adam. Eve ate the fruit and then gave it to Adam, but what would have happened if he had refused to eat? What happened to Eve after she ate the fruit? Nothing! An opportunity to correct her existed, according to the Word of God. Nevertheless, Adam's disobedience to the commandment was willful and wayward.

Adam did not know who the serpent was or what he was to God, but for him to keep the commandment was the hallmark of obedience by faith. Knowing good and evil was useless to Adam. Relying on God's leadership defeats the serpent's schemes, because compliance is better than sacrifice. Obedience to God shuts Satan out.

Satan preys on man's subjectivity, knowing that it's an area of weakness. He influences the conscious mental state of God's people and keeps them from prospering because of the lack of truth. Emotions cause physiological and behavioral actions that stem from strong, subjective, unbiased feelings that create a specific character. So Satan's scheme is to figure out God's calls toward an emotion to justify the physical reactions by applying the knowledge of good and evil based on man's subjectivity.

The devil, Satan, is a liar. He doesn't want us to do what the Spirit of God instructs us to do, but to go against the commands of God—disbelief, discredit, distrust, doubt, mistrust, skepticism, suspicion, uncertainty, denial, rejection, repudiation, unfaithfulness, disbelieving, discounting, and negation.

God created man to lead and gave him a commandment to guide him in his leadership. He told man that he could eat freely from every tree in the garden except the Tree of Knowledge of Good and Evil. There was an excellent reason for this commandment, and it came with severe consequences. The commandment sustained life, and for disobeying the commandment, God said, "thou shalt surely die." (Genesis 2:17)

Thou refer to all of us. God is speaking to Adam as the leader of his descendants, and we are his descendants. When God uses the word, *thou*, He means that all of creation, including you and me, will die if we disobey His commandments. To remove any ambiguity about the consequence of violating this command, God said, "Thou shall." In other words, death is inevitable, so we should expect it to happen. We're all going to die.

Because the devil is a liar, he's prone to steal, kill, and destroy. A lie is a statement known by its maker to be untrue and meant to deceive, distort, exaggerate, defame, slander, and misinform. Satan can and will twist the truth in a scheme to turn us from God. This kind of behavior is typical of Satan. No matter the cost, his goal is to cause God's creation, man and woman, to fail. Failure to uphold God's ultimate purpose in the realm of time leads to eternal spiritual damnation. Beware.

In the Old Testament era, the Spirit of God operated at opportune moments using people whom He'd chosen before the foundation of the world to fulfill His purpose. Expectations are learned and based upon the past, the now, determining the future. Expectations are not justified by the before, so if we've not learned, we've erred and the function is reinstituted. The desired results accomplished will be according to God's standards. If the task has been deemed impossible mathematically and cannot be scientifically achieved, or there is no logical process of explaining, then the odds are that the mission is unrealizable. Then the nonsensical tasks are truly realized, and God's divine powers are discovered, promising patronage, strength, and influence.

God authenticates undisputable facts beyond man's capabilities for an outward sign, an open acknowledgment, for the public profession of his power that He lives and rules firsthand. Then the Word of God, the Bible, is affirmed as authentic and genuine, as attested in the scriptures.

Prophet Moses: The Mosaic Law

Moses was born a Hebrew but raised as an Egyptian by an Egyptian woman. Moses's mother, a Hebrew slave, feared for his life because he was a boy child. So she put him in a basket and placed it in the river, hoping someone would discover him. Pharaoh's daughter found him and claimed him as her child, but she could not nurse Moses, so his own mother was selected to nurse the baby. Moses was saved and nursed from the breast of his mother. When he had grown up, he secretly watched Hebrew slaves toil under the watchful eyes of Egyptian soldiers. One day Moses saw an Egyptian soldier strike a Hebrew slave. Remembering that he was a Hebrew in Egypt, Moses killed the Egyptian soldier and buried him in the sand. Little did Moses know that someone saw him, after which he feared for his life. Pharaoh heard about Moses killing the soldier and sought to kill him.

Moses fled Egypt to live in the land of Midian, as the children of Israel continued to suffer in bondage and cried out to God. God heard their groaning and remembered His covenant—His binding agreement with Abraham, Isaac, and Jacob—that He would not destroy the children of Israel or cast them from His presence. God looked upon the children and had respect for them.

Moses had become a shepherd tending his father-in-law Jethro's flock on the mountain of Horeb. While caring for the flock, Moses saw a bush burning but not being consumed. The angel of the Lord appeared to him amid the flames of the bush. Moses was dumbfounded and curious about what he was seeing: the bush burning but not being consumed. He was investigating closer when he heard the voice of God calling to him from the bush, ". . . Moses, Moses, he said, Here am I." (Exodus 3:4)

Moses hid his face because he was afraid to look upon God. Then God let Moses know He had seen the affliction of His people in Egypt. God also heard the cries of the people and was aware of the cruelty towards them. He knew their sorrows. God came down to earth to deliver His people out of the hand of the Egyptians and to bring them out of that land. Moses is chosen to lead God's people into a good land, a land flowing with milk and honey. God saw the methods of oppression the Egyptians used to oppressed His people. God revealed this to Moses because He wanted Moses to go to Pharaoh with a message and lead the children of Israel out of Egypt. Furthermore, God would be with him, and when Moses had brought the people out, he would serve God upon the mountain of Horeb.

Naturally, Moses asked God what he should say to the Egyptians. God told him to tell the Egyptians that the God of Moses fathers sent him. Now, filled with uncertainty, the Egyptians are going to want to know God's name; so, Moses asked, "what should he say?"

"And God said unto Moses, I AM THAT I AM: and he said, thus shalt thou say unto the children of Israel, I AM hath sent me unto you." (Exodus 3:14) God gave Moses these specific instructions what to say to the Egyptian authorities and to the children of Israel.

Moses did not doubt God, but he was concerned for the people. His biggest concern was whether the Egyptian authorities would believe him and free God's people. Perplexed, he stood there holding the rod used to direct the herd. When God asked what he had in his hand, Moses replied that it was a rod. God told Moses to put the rod on the ground, and when he did, the rod became a snake. Moses ran away from it, but God told him to take the snake by the tail. So Moses did, and the snake became a rod again. Then God told Moses to put his hand into his bosom, and when he took it out, it was leprous as snow. But after settling his hand back against his chest, Moses saw that it had turned back to normal flesh.

Then Moses posed another dilemma to God, a speech problem. He told God that he couldn't express himself clearly enough to do what God was instructing him to do.

The power that God displayed to Moses was far out of the ordinary. Within Moses's mind, a complex psychological battle raged between his consciousness and emotions. Only Moses could explain the real reason for his reluctance. Spiritual warfare is fought within the mind, and the campaigns are supported and strengthened by strong, unpleasant emotions caused by the anticipation or awareness of danger.

Remember, Moses had killed an Egyptian soldier, and Pharaoh was seeking to avenge the soldier's death. Moses had fled Egypt to escape death, so he was torn between avoiding Pharaoh and serving God. Death is real and final, and the prospect of returning to Egypt triggered complicated emotions in Moses. With an attitude of inferiority, he was reluctant to do the work God had designed for him, whether because of cowardice, slothfulness, or unbelief. Moses attributed his reluctance to his tendency to stutter, combined with a fear of speaking in public. He was well educated about the Egyptians. Was the problem really that he was listening to the voice of God's enemy?

Whether Moses really felt inferior to the task or was simply scared, God was not pleased. Moses had a great deal of wisdom and true worth, though maybe a slow tongue. God sometimes chooses as his messengers, people who have few advantages of art or nature, so that his grace in them may appear the more glorious. God sent Aaron to meet Moses, and the more they saw God's bringing them together as a strength, the more pleasant their interview was. Though he could speak well, Aaron could not speak to purpose unless God gave constant teaching and help, for without the continued aid of divine grace, the best gifts will fail. But the tongue of Aaron, when combined with the head and heart of Moses, would prove complete and fit for this errand, and God promised that He would be with them.

Moses reluctant mannerism angered God. So, God shared with Moses that Moses brother Aaron spoke well. When the two of them got together, Moses would be glad of their meeting because Aaron would be the spokesman for Moses. Moses would tell Aaron what God said to say to the Egyptian whereby Aaron would be the deliver, but Moses would be the stead of God. Moses would take the rod of God in his hand, and he shall do the signs and wonders of God before the Egyptians. Still fear plagued Moses concerning the Egyptians who were out to kill him to avenge Moses killing an Egyptian soldier so then God calm his fear by telling him all the men who wanted to kill him were already dead.

Everything about Moses meeting Aaron and telling him about God's assignment happened just as God had said. Moses and Aaron gathered the elders of the children of Israel, and Aaron spoke all the words God had spoken to Moses, and Moses did the signs in the sight of the people, who believed and worshipped God.

Moses then conveyed God's message to Pharaoh, but Pharaoh told him that he didn't know the voice of God, and that he was not letting the children of Israel go. At the same time, Pharaoh increased the Hebrews' workload and stopped providing straw for the making of bricks, which meant they had to go out and retrieve straw themselves. The taskmasters threatened the Hebrews with violence if their production diminished, and the slaves were beaten to secure the threat. The slaves brought the charge of violence against Moses and Aaron for doing the work of the Lord, though Pharaoh's rebellion toward God had initiated him to levy these more stringent burdens on the slaves. Moses, feeling their pain, took the matter before God with a heavy heart.

Moses shared the pain and suffering of the people, along with his own sore displeasure in God. Moses's ignorance of God's plan had been evident when God spoke to him that day in Egypt. Pharaoh was not going to free the Hebrews unless a mighty hand compelled him.

God said to Moses, "and I have heard the groaning of the children of Israel whom the Egyptians keep in bondage; and I have remembered my covenant. Wherefore say unto the children of Israel, I am the LORD, and I will bring them out from under the burdens of the Egyptians, and I will rid you out of their bondage, and I will redeem you with a stretched-out arm, and with significant judgments: I will take you to me for a people, and I will be to you a God: and ye shall know that I am the Lord your God, which bringeth you out from under the burdens of the Egyptians. And I will bring you in unto the land, concerning the which I did swear to give to Abraham, to Isaac, and to Jacob; and I will give it you for a heritage: I am the Lord. (Exodus 6:5 – 8)

Moses took this message to the children of Israel, but they

refused to listen. God also told Moses to carry this message to Pharaoh: "Let My people go." (Exodus 9:1)

To Pharaoh, Moses was made a god and Aaron a prophet by God. Moses was instructed to speak all that God had commanded. Aaron was to speak to Pharaoh that Pharaoh send the children of Israel out of his land. The irony was God hardened Pharaoh's heart that he would refuse to obey Aaron so that God's powers through Moses could be realized. God multiplied His signs and wonders establishing Himself through man to man.

God esteemed Moses and Aaron in their role as instruments for His purpose. He also blessed them for their obedience by allowing them to see power in the signs; signs and wonders to which to the accomplishment in the future for His purpose. The roles of Moses as a god to Pharaoh and Aaron as Moses's prophet serving to establish God on earth. God said, Let us make man in our image, after our likeness: and let them have dominion over the fish of the sea, and over the fowl of the air, and over the cattle, and over all the earth, and over every creeping thing that creep upon the earth. God created man in his own image, in the image of God created he him; male and female created he, them. (Genesis 1:24, 25)

God spoke to Moses, and Moses spoke to Aaron, and Aaron spoke to Pharaoh. Moses conveyed signs of God's power to Pharaoh, as God had instructed him to do. Frogs and lice covered the land, and Pharaoh pledged to free the Hebrews, but he didn't. Then a swarm of flies corrupted the land, and after Pharaoh met certain obligations, God removed the flies. But after the flies were gone, Pharaoh refused to free the slaves again.

Pharaoh deceived Moses and Aaron because his heart was still hard. He had no idea they were messengers of the true and living

God, who had created heaven and earth. The Creator is omnipresent, omniscient, and powerful over all things. Nobody can measure God's purpose or infinite power and wisdom.

Moses and Aaron did all God's signs and wonders before Pharaoh, but God had hardened Pharaoh's heart so that he could not let the children of Israel leave Egypt. So God sent Moses and Aaron back into the land of Egypt, and this time they were significant in the land in the sight of Pharaoh's servants and the view of the people.

God caused more plagues to come into the land and disrupted the lives of the people. The truth of God and His Word was being realized among the people. But still Pharaoh could not release the children of Israel because of his hardened heart. For Moses, the Lord brought one more plague upon Pharaoh and Egypt that surely would compel Pharaoh to thrust Moses and the children of Israel out of his land altogether. With this plague, all the first born from Pharaoh to the maidservants and of all the beast shall die. There shall be a great cry throughout all the land of Egypt, such as there has never been and shall never be any more.

The Passover was Established

The heart is the hub of our human personality. Its where we produce the things we would ordinarily attribute to the mind. Grief, desire, joy, understanding, thought, reasoning, and most importantly, faith and belief are all products of the heart. The heart is the place where God meets us, the container where the truth is stored for good and evil. Whatever is in the heart, the mouth speaks, so the heart is where issues begin and are resolved. There truth is exchanged for a lie, and good is exchanged for evil, but recognizing correct information is the work of God.

How we handle truth produces a consequence; truth and consequences go together. Remember, God has said that we are His children if we obey His commandments, but if we are disobedient, we are not His. People who choose to exercise their own judgment of good and evil obtain a debased mind and are not God's children. Their minds can't discern what is right, accurate, or sound, and they are morally corrupt and deprived of good judgment. They are given over to a debased mind, which is not a punishment; it is a consequence in the here and now. Godless and wicked people who suppress the truth are eventually given over to the sinful desires of their hardened hearts, and thus godlessness consequences occur.

Moses and Aaron, following God's instructions, told all the congregations of Israel that every man should get a male lamb or goat, one-year-old and without a blemish. The lamb or goat was to be kept until the fourteenth day of the month, at which time the whole assembly of the congregation of Israel would kill their animals on the same evening. They were to take the blood of the animal and put it on the upper door posts on both sides of their houses. Afterward they were to roast the animals and eat them—including the head, legs, and internal parts—that night with unleavened bread and bitter herbs, leaving nothing for the morning. They were to eat with their loins girded, their shoes on their feet, and their staff in hand, and they were to eat in haste. This was the Lord's Passover.

These instructions were specific and had to be adhered to. God gave this commandment affecting Pharaoh and the people of his kingdom. This commandment affected everybody—believers and nonbelievers, obedient and disobedient—whoever was in Egypt.

Everyone would do as Moses and Aaron required of them by faith, for they were hearing from God. God would allow the death angel to pass through Egypt that night and kill all the firstborn in the land, including the firstborn of the beasts, this was the judgment that God had pronounced upon Egypt, signifying that He was Lord.

The blood over the entrance door was to be a token indicating that believers were inside, and they complied with God. When the death angel would see the blood, he would pass over that house, and the plague would not fall upon the occupants. That day would be a memorial, for the people were to retain within their hearts the Passover feast as a faithful reminder commemorating the Hebrews' liberation from slavery in Egypt for generations.

Passover was established through unbelief and disobedience. The consequence occurred at midnight, when the Lord allowed the firstborn in Egypt to die—the firstborn of Pharaoh, all the unbelievers, and the disobedient, including the firstborn of every beast. There was barely a house where no one died. Pharaoh's heart now made soft by what he had witnesses and him having no control over his son's life against God through Moses and Aaron was defeated. The consequences of his willful disobedience that upon the dear life of his most precious son, his damned defeat happened and he called for Moses and Aaron by night, and said, Rise up, and get you forth from among my people, both ye and the children of Israel; and go, serve the Lord, as ye have said. (Exodus 12:31)

As God's people left Egypt, the Lord went before them in a cloud by day and led them by a pillar of fire at night to give them light. The Lord told them to sanctify all the firstborn unto Him, and that whatsoever came through the womb among them, man and beast, was His.

The voice of God today would be a detriment to the sanity of man if our ears could hear it. It would be mentally and physically harmful to the average human and cause educated people to seek rational explanations for supernatural events. The person hearing God's voice without understanding would succumb to their own limited knowledge and the destructive effects of medication, counseling, and confinement.

God is not the author of confusion as we know from his orderly creation. He said that everything He created, even man, was good. He gave man the ability to choose, though God also tells us what to choose. In the garden of Eden, God commanded Adam to eat of the Tree of Life, expecting him to carry out the commandment through teaching, being a strong and an obedient soldier. However, God has never failed to hear the cries of His people, nor has He stopped speaking through people of His choice, thus fulfilling His Word.

God chose Moses to build his most holy faith, despite Moses's lifelong struggles with fear and his inability to speak well. There were other faults with which Moses dealt with which he thought made him unworthy to carry out God's mission and purpose regarding the Egyptians – for God's people. But God's plan was not only for Moses to carry a message to Pharaoh, but for Moses to become His effective and leading spokesman to all men in that time and into the future. As an authoritative revealer of God's will, Moses was a divinely inspired writer, the prophetic writer of the first five books of the Bible, and a messenger to all the world, then and now.

Men and women of the Old Testament era possessed, or sometimes lacked, something unique that made them candidates for God's use. He manifested Himself profoundly in everyone He chose, and when their abilities were used by God, the results were overwhelming, significant, and reliable. These people were prolific believers that God is, and they became prophets who were gifted with extraordinary spiritual and moral insight, conscious of the facts of spiritual truths inspired by God.

Through the prophets, God manifested His Word and established His will for man throughout the land. From His Spirit, man received instructions. The problem was not the prophets, but the people to whom the prophets spoke. Faith comes by hearing the Word of God, and without hope, it is impossible to please God. The people lacked confidence.

We are God's people, and since the violation of God's commandment in the garden of Eden, God has been leading His people back to Him. The operative term here is *His people*. God deemed those who kept His commandments His people throughout the Old Testament.

Also, those who lived in the New Testament era and were spiritually born again with the Holy Spirit and accepting Jesus as Lord over their lives, are His people. These people were God's people because God said it, but those who had not the Spirit of Christ were none of His. He said that too.

God's Word establishes belief by faith and His word shall come to pass. Without the profound stature of God today as He appeared in the Old Testament, it is difficult to imagine a living God. Since the early days after Jesus's death, fewer people openly profess themselves to be followers of Jesus or even confess that there is a God.

Today many people rebel and do not believe that a true and living God exists, in spite of the revelations. They practice idolatry with an immoderate attachment to physical objects as their gods, and their resistance to the living God fuels the opposing spirit, that is Satan. Their ignorance of the demonic spirit's influence over them keeps them distracted from the interest God has in them. The prophets convey the proper clarity, outlining processes taught by the Spirit of God to bring into focus, God's supernatural phenomenon, marked by gradual changes that lead toward His intended results according to His will. People must humbly yield to God's superior strength and ability to overpower the appeal of Satan. Hearing the word of God—whether caught, taught, bought, or through prophecy—provides vision to bring God's purpose to light. Just as there are consequences for disobedience, there are also consequences for obedience.

There has been a constant rivalry between right and wrong, good and bad. Individual interpretations significantly manifest behavior based on a particular person's environment which directly influences the activities of that person. How we view right, wrong, good, and bad affects our beliefs, understanding, and choices, which affect our decisions and challenge us to come to God by hope, faith, and trust—doing what is right according to the truth. Strong roots stabilize progressive growth; however, our hearts must be grounded in truth for the gain to be positive. Our sensory and perception abilities to notice and understand things become mentally sharp and intelligent enough not to get caught up emotionally within our issues. Many issues are difficult to deal with and hard inferences are formed without proof or sufficient evidence. These issues become our sources of trouble and worry; nevertheless, truth can and will drive our questions away or cause them to vanish.

The problems of the people in the Old Testament probably

would and could make us candidates for God to use as spokespeople for Him. The people whom God used in the Old Testament had physical, mental cognitive, and developmental conditions that limited their abilities to engage in specific normal tasks. Many of us are experiencing those same issues today, but with a different mindset. The then and the now conditions could not and cannot be corrected by man's intellect, sorcerous rituals, powers of pagan gods, or witchcraft. Nothing known to man will remove or fix these physical and mental disadvantages.

The opposing spirit, Satan, enhances problems to his advantage by inserting into our thoughts ideas that are contrary to the good. Satan reaffirms fear through doubt and depression, and he brings false hope through selfishness. Satan is in opposition to God and he aspire to excel a kingdom higher than God. And as a result, he has been tossed out of the heavenly realm, which is God's kingdom, and into the earthly realm. He retaliates by turning as many souls as possible away from God by lying to us, stealing from us, and causing our premature spiritual and physical death.

Word Through Prophets

In the Old Testament, God used His Spirit to empower people who were either physically or mentally disadvantaged to become spokespeople for Him. He does this spiritually and miraculously so that no human can claim a favorable outcome except by trusting in the truth of the Spirit. The prophets spoke from firsthand knowledge of what the Spirit had said to them concerning those whom God had on His mind. Believe!

God knew us before we were born. Before we were formed in

the womb. God knew everything that would happen to us between birth and death. He knows what He wants to accomplish through us, how to use us, and for what purpose.

God used the prophet Jeremiah's inferiorities to bring him to preach and prophesy. Jeremiah initially resisted the call of God, complaining that he was only a child and did not know how to speak. However, God insisted that Jeremiah go and speak the doctrine which God would teach him, then He touched Jeremiah's mouth to place His word there. At God's command, Jeremiah got ready during his childhood and gained specific mental skills, obtaining readiness and God's grace, including a fearless attitude. He stood up and spoke as he was told, and he went where he was sent.

The word became like fire in Jeremiah's heart. He was unable to hold on to it. He spoke in gatherings to men, women, and children and one on one. He was well trained and fully literate from his earliest preaching, and he became a preaching prophet primarily, teaching throughout Israel and condemning idolatry, greedy priests, and false prophets. Jeremiah became known as the weeping prophet because of the sorrow he felt preaching to a disordered nation that was reluctant to adhere to the messages. The people's reluctance to accept the truth underscored their future tragedy, and that saddened him to tears.

Jeremiah was born during a troubled time in history, and he shed tears over the sins of the people. He called them to repent of their sins so that they might avoid God's judgment. Sadly, their refusal to turn away from idolatry and other sins, their reluctance would bring their destruction from the north, from where they would be invaded. The invasion and destruction occurred because the people had been unfaithful to the laws of God's covenant and had forsaken God through their worshipping false gods. Jeremiah also condemned them for sacrificing their children as offerings to Moloch, a Semitic god.

These people had strayed far from God, causing Him to withdraw His blessings. Jeremiah was guided by God to proclaim that the nation of Judah would face famine and plunder, and they would be taken captive by foreigners who would exile them to a foreign land. The people reduced their values of being related to God and His content of purities and instead increased their sadistic characteristics that ran rampant among the people. They challenged the prophets' messages that it be their will, the people's will, not God's will.

There were many spiritual, intellectual prophets with God's insight who preached, taught, and clearly proved the value in condemning idolatry, greediness, and false prophets.

The prophet Malachi penned the book of Malachi, the last book of the Old Testament. He recorded a debate between the loving Father (God) and His sinful children. God urged His children to change their wicked ways, but they refused, responding instead with fretful complaints and stinging accusations. This debate provided a glimpse into God's passionate love for His people. All the many topics covered in the discussion stemmed from God's desire for His children to reciprocate His love, to exhibit integrity, purity, faithfulness, and justice in their daily lives.

God's final words through Malachi to His children reverberated with hope through God sending the prophet Elijah. Serving as a prophet was about as rough as it got in Israel. A prophet regularly traveled and received little or no pay. The benefits of his divine calling to a religious vocation that didn't take effect until after his death.

Despite these drawbacks, Elijah answered the call to proclaim God's Word to a people who, as often, showed little inclination to hear it.

False prophets surfaced proclaiming to deliver messages they supposedly got from a higher being, God. These prophets would usually say exactly what the people want to hear. Elijah's emotions had run the gamut from the extraordinary thrill of victory to the chilling fear of impending death, from the apex of euphoria to the depths of depression. It was at this point that the Lord intervened. Elijah took cover in a cave as God began an impressive demonstration of His power. First, a rock-splitting wind tore against the mountainside. Then the earth shook with a rumbling earthquake, followed by a raging fire. Finally, Elijah's ringing ears detected a gentle whisper. He stepped out of the cave and heard the voice of God softly demonstrating His real power.

All of God's people might experience the same truth that Elijah learned that day he stepped out of the cave. God, and only God, can turn injustice and evil into praise and victory. Unless we are focused on God's will, we can easily miss His manifestations of power. He can shatter mountains, shake the very foundation of the earth, and rain down fire from heaven, but often He speaks to His beloved in a soft, lilting lover's whisper.

During the storms of life, we need to listen for that same barely audible whisper. We may have to struggle through many difficult days before we quiet down and begin to hear and understand what God is saying. When we get past the events that drain our energy, we are in an excellent place to slow down and reflect on what we've just experienced.

Malachi, the last Old Testament prophet, closed his prophecy with words of hope that would offer a solution to all future generations. After Malachi, there wasn't another divine prophet for decades, and the apparent absence of God's voice affected societal developments. The prophets' teachings gave staunch believers hope for an anticipated messiah. This same hope was extended to those who possessed a lesser faith and or even doubted the existence of a living God. The scarcity of God's divine leadership during the period between the Old and New Testaments catapulted some people into excessive living off the fruits and the labor of others. Where favorable progress was tarnished, the idea of hope became problematic.

Where was the hope Malachi preached? God said that if His commands were adhered to, He would fulfill His promises. Also, God said that a day was coming in which the proud and wicked would be burned up, leaving them no offspring for future generations.

Moses, a Hebrew, was born into slavery under the order of death by a king who feared that a male child would dethrone him. Moses's mother laid him in a basket and put the basket in a river, hoping that a surrogate family would rescue and raise him. He was found by Egyptian royalty, the same people who were supposed to kill him. They employed his natural mother to nurse him, and he lived in the palace of the ruler who had wanted to kill Hebrew male babies at birth. Moses's tenure living as an Egyptian was purposefully designed by God for His purpose to demonstrate to us today that rather than hurting us, He wants us to prosper.

God took the infirmities of a young child, Jeremiah, and miraculously turned the infirmities into what was needed for Jeremiah to glorify Him. The reluctant child was shown that God was real, not just intellectually but by heartfelt revelations to which Jeremiah could personally attest. Nothing less than the power of God was responsible for Jeremiah having an effective outcome. The point of this miracle, although it benefited Jeremiah, was that the people would believe God and become faithful unto a promised hope, trusting His word.

We cannot forget the debate that Malachi had with God's people regarding the promise of hope. This debate provided a glimpse into God's passionate love for His people. God urged His children to change their wicked ways, but they refused, responding instead with fretful complaints and stinging accusations. Because of their acts of defiance, God deemed them to be debased minded, and the consequences of refusing to change their minds and behavior fell upon them.

God's final words through Malachi reverberated with hope through the prophet Elijah. Elijah answered the call to proclaim God's word to the people, and the people refused to hear it. Nevertheless, hope will come if we believe and wait with patience and cheerfulness.

Consider the outcome of all the prophets God sent to show His people the way back to Him. Some people still believed that in time, God's enemy would destroy the minds of the people with lies, greed, and death. Others died with the belief of hope of the words the prophets preached in their hearts never realizing the hope of glory; while some being filled with disparity and lived for the moment.

God said the earthly realm would be destroyed by fire after the time of Noah. He also had Malachi talk to the people about the earth's destruction by fire, remember, God cannot lie. God spoke into existence all creation, and it is so. God was present before the beginning of time before creation. He created heaven and earth. God blessed the seventh day after creating all that was created, and sanctified it, and rested from all His work. God said, "I change not." (Malachi 3:8)

CHAPTER 3

A Time for Silence

Silence speaks louder than words
and is heard more profoundly.
When we add what we
don't hear audibly,
...it's felt in the heart!

THERE WAS A PASTOR WHO drank whiskey, smoked cigarettes, and frequently used profanity fluently and without respect. He was well educated, having earned master's degrees from two prominent universities, and he landed two well-paying positions, one with state government and the other with a local firm. He partied and danced in dance halls and taverns, consuming more and more alcohol as he became more jubilant. The more he drank, the more fun he had, which made him want to drink more. One Sunday, he went to church, and as he listened to the sermon, the Lord spoke into his heart. He sat there in the pulpit and meditated on what was being etched into his heart. After that Sunday, he lost his taste for alcohol, gave up smoking and using profanity, and stopped going to the clubs and dancing. His search for salvation began.

The pastor began genuinely reading and studying God's Word, and at the same time, welcoming the Holy Spirit into his life for guidance. He allowed the Spirit of God to rest within his heart and lead him on the path of righteousness. He truly began to believe Jesus. He trusted the Spirit of God by faith, and God began changing his character to the likeness of Jesus. As time passed, the pastor's aura became completely anew as he spoke of God with scriptural authority and characterizing the things of God out of love for God. He attended seminary college and graduated with the satisfaction that this degree meant more than his previous degrees because this degree marked his dedication to the service for the Lord.

Even though the pastor had given his life to the service of Christ, he still had to deal with issues. He wanted a better job, so he applied for a position in a field of study in which he had a master's degree. As he dressed on the day of his interview, he confidently rehearsed answering the questions that he anticipated as he watched himself in the mirror critiquing his own stamina and professionalism. The job was within his scope of education, he was well-qualified, and possessed experience in the field. He couldn't imagine not being offered this position.

Before the pastor left home for the interview, he took a long look in the mirror to check his appearance. He quickly made a few adjustments to his hair, pulled his coat up over his shoulders, took a deep breath, then sighed with confidence. Praying to the Lord for a successful interview with the guidance of the Holy Spirit, he then thanked God for the job, and he left home.

During the interview, the pastor answered the questions confidently. Relaxed but keeping his composure, he asked pertinent questions to show his interest in the position. He never acted overconfident, thus allowing the interviewer to remain in control. After the interview, the pastor left the room confident and filled with jubilation he'd landed the position. Joy radiated throughout his body, he believed that he had nailed the interview and the job was all his.

Several days later, he received a call that the job had been offered to another candidate and the candidate accepted the job. The caller extended his appreciated to the pastor for his participation in the search and the call ended. The news was disappointing, even heartbreaking. The pastor thought back over the interview to see where he had gone wrong, but he could not see any problems. He pondered over and over the scenario and saw no reason why he did not get the position. So he dismissed the ordeal with, "Oh well," and continued to hold God in high esteem as he went about his travels.

Several weeks later, the pastor met the person who had been given the job, an acquaintance and he learned that the job's workload was heavy and required much time, effort, and attention. This person was miserable. Problems begun to plague him. In a short, the demanding position had produced debilitating stress that was threatening the man's physical and mental health.

Had this been a setup by the enemy to thwart the service of God for the pastor? Only God has the answer. Nevertheless, the Spirit of God intervened and the pastor had not gotten the job which would have hindered his ability to serve God in the ministry.

Today the work mandated by God for the children of God will continue. This was made possible by a new and better covenant made by God to implement the hope that the prophet Malachi preached. God revealed Himself to the pastor through the intervention of the Holy Spirit by loving him enough to care for him not to lead him into temptation. The pastor knows that God intervened and saved him from a job that would have kept him from serving God in the capacity in which God desired. Now he serves God with spiritual and intellectual depth, insight, and understanding that he shares with others by preaching with wisdom, power, and authority about the goodness of God.

Timing

Why is it important to listen to God without grumbling? In the world, the heart is thought to be the command post of life's issues, and actions and behaviors are said to flow directly from it. God's Word frequently describes the condition of the heart, from where all issues flow. While God's people were enslaved in Egypt, Pharaoh's heart was described as hard. As a result, he would not listen to God, who spoke through Moses and Aaron, in spite of the demonstrations of supernatural power that he witnessed.

King David, a man after God's heart, had a son, Solomon,

who was meant to inherit the throne after King David's death. Although King Solomon started strong leading his kingdom by believing in God, but he became foolish. Solomon began guiding his kingdom by prayer, worship, and witnessing what God manifest to him through the Spirit. Solomon prospered his kingdom on proven grounds stemming from his father, King David's relationship with God through the knowledge of God's faithfulness. As Solomon grew old, his wives turned his heart after pagan gods, and his heart was not fully devoted to the living God and disaster came upon his kingdom.

Ananias and Sapphira sold a parcel of their land, and then each separately lied to the Holy Spirit about the sale holding back some of the proceeds from the sale. Their hearts were filled with deceit by the spirit of Satan to keep back part of the money. The lies they told resulted in their deaths neither of them knowing the other lied and died. The heart of man dies spiritually and /or physically when it is contrary to what is righteous.

Hard hearts, wandering hearts, boastful hearts, arrogant hearts, lying hearts—there seems to be no end to the corruption of which the human heart is capable. Our hearts are so insidious because of someone else who has a heart problem: Satan himself.

Our hearts are the center of our very being and carry emotions that feel good when we derive pleasure through sight, touch, smell, taste, and hearing. Also, the heart uses emotion to filter hurt by these same senses. Satan attacks the mind with lies and deceit, which have a gradual and cumulative influence on how the heart reacts toward the senses, thereby creating belief. Our minds, independent of the heart, rule our emotions with outside stimuli, and our actions are characterized by that stimuli.

Satan boasted, he would ascend in the heavenly realm. He would raise his throne above the stars of God. This attitude got him kicked out of the heavenly realm. Satan presumed that he could raise himself above God, but since he was kicked out of heaven, Satan has set out to convince humans that they, too, could achieve this godlike status. His scheme in the garden of Eden achieved his dastardly purpose, and he has tempted others to buy into a lie ever since.

Is there a cure for a deceitful heart? Yes, the cure is truth! We too were ignorant, foolish, disobedient, deceived, and enslaved by all kinds of passions and pleasures. We live with malice and envy, being hated and hating one another. God, our Father, who has loved us from the beginning of time, will always love us and wants us to spend eternity with Him. Our God will always love us with the same kind of love He possessed before creation, because it's in His character to love.

God chose to reveal Himself through the nation of Israel, which seems to be a hard concept for many people to understand. To be chosen because of God's love, grace, and faithfulness is indeed a great privilege and honor, but with it comes great responsibility. Israel is often referred to as the chosen people or nation, which might suggest that God has historically preferred and favored one nation or people over all others. However, the wider context shows that from the beginning, God planned to use Israel as a light and a blessing to all nations, and ultimately all nations are to follow as God's people. He chose Israel not because He decided to redeem every Israelite, but because He decided to use Israel to play an important role in bringing about redemption for the entire world. Ultimately God chose Israel to be His chosen people for the purpose of producing the Messiah. The Messiah had to come from some nation of people, and God chose Israel. God calls Israel to a higher standard precisely because of His unique revelation and choice of them.

The Israelites are part of a family tree that goes all the way back to the first humans on earth. God chose the lineage of Abraham, Isaac, and Jacob because a nation of people would come from them and serve as a light and a blessing to other nations. Their God, the same God, emphasize the covenant He made first with Abraham and repeated it with the following generations. The Israelites serve as an example, a lesson to the world that trees bear up under storms and their branches are subjected to adversity. The adherence to truth profits the Spirit. The truth triumphs over our flesh and the forces of the mind. Our souls can sustain God's grace for generations by faith through teaching.

Jeremiah, a major prophet, was called to prophesy about Jerusalem's destruction by invaders. Through his prophecies, Jeremiah warned the people that if they did not repent and turn back to God, the city would face inevitable punishment. Israel had been unfaithful to the laws of the covenant and had forsaken God by worshipping Baal. By refusing to keep the covenant of God, they refused to walk in His law and forgot the works and wonders that He had shown them. They had provoked God in the wilderness and grieved Him in the desert. Again and again they tempted God. Time after time they limited the Holy One of Israel not remembering His power. They revoked the highest God by not keeping His testimonies. They turned back to their foolish ways and acted unfaithfully like their earthly fathers, reverencing other gods. They began walking in the statutes of the nations whom the Lord had cast out from the children of Israel.

Israel was sinning against the God who had brought them out

of the land of Egypt. So God rejected all the descendants of Israel, afflicted them, and delivered them into the hands of plunderers until He had cast them from His sight. In doing so, God was completely faithful to the children of Israel, because that's exactly what He had promised He would do if they persistently sinned against Him. At the right time and for the right people, God will hone His unconditional promises to the patriarchs. Israel's sad history is the consequence of the people's faithlessness, not of God's weakness.

God miraculously prepared Jeremiah from birth, in the eyes of the people. He put words of wisdom in Jeremiah's mouth, and Jeremiah delivered those words as God gave him utterance. When Jeremiah wept excessively and earnestly, not in affectation but out of sincerity and honesty. His weeping had no effect on the people's belief that God was truly on the scene. The patriarchs were faithful, as God attested again and again, but because of the people's recalcitrance, God withheld His blessings, ultimately separating Himself from the Israelites by casting them out of the land He had promised to the patriarchs.

God punished Israel for its disobedience by deferring the fulfillment of His promises to the patriarchs. This deferment did not make God unfaithful to the people, because His promises to them had been conditional, based on their obedience to His revelation. The Israelites continued worshipping idol gods, lying, and cheating, the greedy priests kept on lying and stealing until they made yokes of iron for themselves. God put that yoke upon them. The promise of God still stood for the chosen nation because God does not lie. The conditions still stood also; if they would repent and pray, He would hear them.

God has given us dominion over the earth and the will to

choose. God created an environment conducive to supporting and encourage learning. He set a high standard offering education and training in the crucial developmental period of our early days. During that time, we are supported and encouraged by God's Spirit to become spiritual beings having a human experience. The early time in life is crucial for guidance toward adulthood for the human experience as people emerge from adolescence. Understanding the developmental challenges with new identities while relating with people are important processes that can be misconstrued.

During the rearing time in early life, we are named and branded—given nicknames, sick names, and called all kinds of off-colored names as society's way of preying on us. We are fed all kinds of truths—that is, lies made to disguise the truth to some people, the same being untruths to others which is reflected by the names we are called. We come out of the womb into abnormalities that are perceived normal and those abnormalities are normalized by parents who are not perfect. Depending on the environment in which we are reared, the names and labels might be forced upon us, and we adopt them and become the labels. We answer to the name that we are called, and that is who we become internally good, mediocre, or bad.

A black couple was shopping in a grocery store. As they started up one aisle, a little white boy, about six years old, came running toward them from the other end of the same aisle. Looking up, the boy saw the black couple and put on the brakes. He began to slide toward them. Startled, and with a slight grin, he began backing up. Turning to his mother behind him, he said, "Look, Momma, those are niggers. Daddy calls them spades."

What makes you right or wrong? Can your environment say that you are right or wrong? Yes, it can. But what about the timing as related to belief? Can timing influence belief? Belief is paramount, and inducement spurs desired outcomes. Is what is taught to be right actually right? Can right or wrong be wrong or right within an environment until our heart tells us something is right or wrong? When you were a child, did anyone ever tell you that if you broke a mirror, you would have seven years of bad luck? Would you have to bury a piece of the glass to thwart off the bad luck!

Timing and Belief

In the Old Testament days lived the prophet Daniel. As a young man, Daniel had demonstrated the wisdom of God and matured beyond his years. He was intimately acquainted with God, who revealed deep and hidden things to him. Daniel's dedication to God was an outward expression of an inward belief, and his commitment was thorough and regular. He worshipped and prayed to God, and the people esteemed him highly, marking his character faithful with respect.

When faced with impossible circumstances, it was how Daniel viewed God that mattered, rather than what the issues were or whether the odds seemed to be against him. When he was in his eighties, he provided the people with important reminders of God's promise that one day God would send a messiah in the face of their captivity. God wanted the Israelites to realize that He had not abandoned them. He would, in fact, care for them and protect them until the coming of His Anointed One. So Daniel taught a message of obedience, trust, and belief, while at the same time refusing the name of Belteshazzar and the meat of the king so that he didn't defile himself.

Three other men also had no blemishes and were well favored

and skillful in all wisdom, understanding, and science—Hananiah, Mishael, and Azariah. Exercising his power, the king changed their names: Hananiah to Shadrach, Mishael to Meshach, and Azariah to Abednego. Shadrach, Meshach, and Abednego were children of Israel and of the king's seed, so they were apt to teach.

God gave His creation the power and right to govern and control themselves. He made His creation sovereign with authority, dominion, and a will to choose above all other creatures.

God humanized man. Life invariable brings fiery trials, and during the crises, we can cling to the promise that God is walking with us. There is no circumstance, trial, or pending decision in which God is not present as our helper, blocking Satan from getting to us. Because of the hardness of people hearts, some people cannot hear the voice of God, so they cannot and will not reign victorious against the ruler of darkness, Satan.

We have no control over time. We fight every minute of the day and night, struggling with life issues to survive. We must fight, physically and mentally, the issues we see and those we do not see. We fight Satan blindly, as though in an arena, with no control over time, with weapons which we are unfamiliar, and against issues we don't fully understand. We don't know Satan's methodology or sense of timing. How can we fight Satan if we don't know when, where, or how he's coming after us? How can we fight him if we don't even know that we're in a fight? Can we fight a spirit? How do we get the better of someone if we don't know the rules of the game? We need God!

Daniel was charged with the impossible task of interpreting King Nebuchadnezzar's troubling dream. The king summoned magicians, astrologers, and sorcerers and commanded them to show him his dream and what his dream meant. If they failed, they would be cut into pieces and their homes made into dunghills. If they interpreted the dream correctly, their reward would be gifts of great honor. The magicians, astrologers, and sorcerers requested that the king reveal the dream to them, and then they would supply the interpretation. The problem was the king could not remember the dream, not one detail of the dream. He wanted them to envision the dream as he had experienced it, and then interpret it to him. Impossible? They told him that there wasn't anyone who could show the king his dream, and that no king, lord, or ruler would ask such a thing. This angered the king so much that he ordered all the wise men in Babylon destroyed. Death loomed over the king's magicians, astrologers, and sorcerers. The impossible was asked of them and they knew they could not deliver to the king the interpretation of what the king could not remember.

The wise men sought out Daniel, who told his companions Hananiah, Mishael, and Azariah that they should pray for God's mercy so that they wouldn't perish with the rest of the wise men. They knew there was a God in heaven who revealed secrets.

Daniel, Hananiah, Mishael, and Azariah all prayed. The dream was revealed to Daniel in a night vision. Daniel blessed God's name, for wisdom and might are God's. God changes the times and the seasons, giving wisdom to the wise and knowledge to those who know understanding. God reveals the deep things, the secrets, and He knows what is in the dark. Daniel told the king about his dream and its interpretation.

We cannot control timing, but only our beliefs. God has supplied a cloud of witnesses among the Old Testament people to prove that He is real. Throughout the Old Testament period, testimonies circulated about a living God whose miracles were marveled by witnesses who could not dispute the truth of a living God. Still some people hearts remained hard with unbelief and doubt. They praised men in power who worshipped idols that didn't approve or disapprove of anything. We have no power or authority to control or guide time, we can operate in time and control our beliefs with the help of God through the Holy Spirit.

King Nebuchadnezzar made a golden image and asked princes, governors, captains, judges, treasurers, counselors, sheriffs, and other rulers of the provinces to gather for its dedication. It was announced that anyone who did not bow down and worship the image would be cast into a burning fiery furnace. A decree was issued commanding that every person—at the sound of the cornet, flute, harp, sackbut, psaltery, dulcimer, or any other musical instrument—should bow and worship the golden image. Anyone who failed to do so would be cast into a fiery furnace.

Shadrach, Meshach, and Abednego, were Jewish and had been given charge over the affairs of the province of Babylon. At the sound of the musical instruments, they all refused to bow to worship the golden image of the king. On hearing about this, King Nebuchadnezzar became enraged and asked them himself if they refused to worship his golden image. Apparently not receiving a favorable answer, he made sure that he had heard them right and that they understood the consequences. The king reiterated his decree and warned them if they refused to worship his image, they would be cast into the fiery furnace. He asked them what god would deliver them out of his hands?

They humbly answered, "we are not careful to answer thee in this matter. If it be so, our God whom we serve is able to deliver us from the burning fiery furnace, and he will deliver us out of thine hand, O king. But if not, be it known unto thee, O king, that we will not serve thy gods, nor worship the golden image thou hast set up." (Daniel 3:16, 17, 18)

Now full of fury, Nebuchadnezzar commanded that the furnace be heated seven times hotter than it was. He commanded Shadrach, Meshach, and Abednego to be bound and cast into the fiery furnace.

The fiery furnace which was exceedingly hot. The flames killed the men who took Shadrach, Meshach, and Abednego to the furnace. Still bound, Shadrach, Meshach, and Abednego fell into the middle of the fire.

Astonished, the king rushed to the furnace, opened it, peered inside, and asked his counselors, "Did we cast three bound men into the fire?"

They answered, "True, O king."

Still astonished, the king replied, "I see four men walking, freely and unharmed, in the midst of the fire. That fourth man looks like the Son of God."

Then he called to Shadrach, Meshach, and Abednego, "You servants of the highest God, come here."

The three men did so, and the princes, governors, captains, and counselors all saw that the fire had not harmed Shadrach, Meshach, and Abednego. They had no singed hair, their coats were not burned, and they didn't smell of fire or smoke.

Nebuchadnezzar announced his astonishment in the presence of the princes and the prime ministers of the state. He confessed praise and glory to the true God, who gained his trust through ingenuity and with compelling evidence, without argument from him.

Despite the force of his conviction, his conversion did not appear to be thorough. He did not relinquish his gods and the worship of them, saying blessed be the God of Shadrach, Meshach, and Abednego. Nebuchadnezzar did not refer to God as his own God, but as the God of Daniel who sent His angel and delivered His servants who trusted in Him.

Nebuchadnezzar called the fourth man he saw in the furnace an angel of God, Jesus Christ. The Son of God was sent by His divine Father to rescue Shadrach, Meshach, and Abednego from being consumed in the fire. Because of their confidence in God, whom the king now remembers and observes, a distinction before the people was realized there is a living God who they can call upon to deliver them.

After seeing Shadrach, Meshach, and Abednego's devotion and obedience to God, the king canceled his decree regarding worshipping his idol. The refusal of Shadrach, Meshach, and Abednego to obey the king's command, knowing it was their duty to obey God rather than man, persuaded the king to change his command. After that, instead of obliging them to worship his image, the king blessed their God.

The king was overwhelmed at Shadrach, Meshach, and Abednego's willingness to freely give up their lives, without any resistance, into the hands of those who were ordered by the king to cast them into the furnace. They readily yielded themselves so that they do not serve or worship any god except their own living God. They chose to deliver themselves to death in the furnace rather than serve any other god than the God of Israel. Such was their hearts constancy with firmness of mind that their attachment to the true God, and their faithfulness to Him would prevail.

Timing and belief are surely in God's hand. The king had

assembled the authoritative figures of his council to demonstrate his power and to make examples of the laypeople. This form of power is bullying. It is demonstrated for to make an example of disobedience to witnesses. The golden graven image was a symbol of pride, and the king wanted it to be worshipped and respected as a god.

Shadrach, Meshach, and Abednego were favored and skillful in all wisdom and understanding in the science by God. They honored the living God constantly by praying, developing a relationship by faith, trust, and obedience to God's will that He is faithful.

God used this functional scheme of Satan to show the king, his council, and all the people who gathered the results of the king's dysfunctional disobedience toward God's word. They all had preconceived notions of the misery Shadrach, Meshach, and Abednego would endure as they burned to death, but they didn't know the power of the goodness of the true and living God. They witnessed the heat that radiated from the furnace, which killed the attendants, and yet the fire inside the furnace did nothing to Shadrach, Meshach, and Abednego.

The crowd was in awe. An emotion that irrefutably originated in the heart and then came from the mouth. Remember, issues in life come from the heart, and the mouth speaks what is in the heart. This episode of God's power is impossible to refute. Here the living God obtained respect and inspired through the dignity of wisdom, dedication, trust, and obedience by faith. Shadrach, Meshach, and Abednego possessed strong feelings of reverential fear and respect for God at His word. Their reverential fear inspired the people regarding nature's wonders and filled their hearts with the sacred authority of God, which put an end to Satan's scheme for some.

When the king looked into the furnace and saw four when there should have been three, he confessed that the fourth looked like the Son of God. No man told him this; this was inspired by authority, by the Spirit of God.

We see that nothing could have been done concerning time. This episode in life happened when it happened. God orchestrates all elements of time. We cannot recover time, so we must use it wisely while we can operate in it. We can control our belief by relying on the Helper, and then Truth will steer us in the correct direction, putting us on the journey back to God. God will always love us, but we must be obedient to His word by faith, trusting in Him and worshipping Him. We must worship God in spirit and truth.

The Spirit of God was present then, as He is now. The difference then was that God used prophets to guide mankind, and the prophets did what He inspired them to do. Some heard God's message and believed, others heard and doubted, and the rest just refused to believe, no matter what. God manipulated man through time, eradicating generations of people and their offspring, yet disobedience was still prevalent.

Time and Silence

No person was born with an innate sense of survival. When a newborn enters this world, it must be taught life skills as it grows toward maturity. This requires people to teach, but the teaching should incorporate the qualities of God whereby we speak things into existence through the power of words through belief and faith. Eventually, people become lackadaisical about the teachings of the power in the spoken word, and then began refusing to trust. People started patterning themselves after other people trying futilely to achieve their goals in their own strength.

Then is God silent, or did people stop listening? God never stopped teaching! People turn away from God to worship wooden heads on poles, stone figures, and men who support false assertions and worshipping idols. People even worship sacred items in the belief that luck will prevail, the rabbit's foot! Meanwhile God waits patiently. The Spirit of God keeps speaking, keeps on teaching and waiting for people to turn to Him. Remember, God's in eternity, and we're in time! Time for us runs out, but how does time affect God?

How does time compare with eternity?

> Time is the indefinite continued progress of existence and events that occur in apparently irreversible succession from the past, through the present, to the future. It is a component quantity of various measurements used to sequence events, to compare the duration of events or the intervals between them, and to quantify rates of change of quantities in material reality or in the conscious experience ... Time has long been an important subject of study in religion, philosophy, and science, but defining it in a manner applicable to all fields without circularity has consistently eluded scholars. (Wikipedia, s.v. "Time," https://en.wikipedia.org/wiki/Time)

Eternity means infinite or unending time, and being eternal means not having a beginning or an end. God is eternal, residing in eternity. Eternity has generally been considered as divisible into two parts: eternity a parte ante (past eternity), and eternity a parte post (future eternity). We were not living before eternity nor can we live after eternity therefore time is between the two points of the extremes. At some point in time we are born and at some other point in time, we are going to die. Is it possible to live on the post end of eternity?

Eternity past encompasses creation in the Old Testament era. Time comes into play in the four hundred years of silence between Malachi and the New Testament prophet Matthew. Since time represents a measurement, then today will become yesterday as we look forward to eternity past, which is tomorrow. But was God silent during the four hundred years between the Old and New Testaments?

God warned the Israelites, through the prophets teaching them and showing them God's unmatchable powers and that He is the only living God. Today, the believer need not fear the fiery trials of afflictions and temptations by which the Savior refines His people because we have a God who change not. We are not consumed by the world and Satan's schemes because God's compassion has not failed, we are not of the world. The lessons were and is irrefutable, and God's word is sound, we have eternal souls.

Finally, through Malachi, the people learned God's warning were both profitable and damning. Evil pursues sinners. Remember, God is unchangeable, and though the sentence against evil workers may not be executed speedily, it will be executed. The Lord is as much an enemy to sin as ever.

Generations of people living within the Old Testament era had turned away from God and not kept His commandments. They showed great perverseness in sin and made excuses not to separate themselves from their sin. Nevertheless, just as evil communications corrupt good minds and manners, good communications also confirm them, and a book of remembrance was written before God that whosoever was of good communications should be vessels of mercy. God will take care that His children not perish. Everyone is either righteous or wicked, based on whether they serve God, and everyones soul is going to either eternal heaven or eternal hell.

The silence of God to the prophets in the Old Testament period was caused by the people's dismal attitudes and their lack of courage to see beyond the obstacles in their lives. They hindered themselves by failing to acknowledge the presence and power of God.

People will lie for any reason if doing so benefits their agenda. Cain slew his brother Abel because of low self-esteem. He was given the same command that was given to Abel, but because Cain chose not to abide by God's commandment, and God acknowledged Abel through his obedience, Cain killed Abel.

Abel was a herder and Cain was a farmer. They were both good at their jobs. Cain brought the Lord an offering of fruit, and Abel brought an offering of the fat firstlings of his flock. The Lord respected Abel and his offering. The Lord had no respect for Cain's offering. The Lord's rejecting Cain's offering upset him and he became angry.

The problem was the difference in the two offerings. God is God, and He respected Abel and his offering over Cain's offering. This shows us that it is God's plan to bring us to an expected end according to the plans He has for us. Cain did not know the significance of God's plan, and his emotions rose after God had no respect for his offering. When Cain got upset, God's enemy was allowed into his thoughts, and Cain shut God out. He didn't understand God's plan for him, and he killed Abel.

This type of sickness promoted by Satan, plagued the Old Testament era. The prophets could not reach all the people, even with all of God's promotions. Malachi preached that a day was coming when proud wicked people would be burned to stubble. He reassured them that our Lord had told him this and that the burning would not leave a branch or root behind. Those who are righteous shall arise with healing wings and tread upon the wicked, and our Lord shall make this happen.

Malachi referred the people to the law of Moses, the statutes and judgments that make up the law for Israel. God also established a time for the judgment, He was sending Elijah the prophet before the great and dreadful day of the Lord. In the day of the Lord, the Lord shall turn the hearts of the fathers to the children, and the hearts of the children to their fathers.

The opposite of the irony of Cain and Abel is that God would bring a point of agreement into His timing. He said, "Behold I will send you Elijah," meaning one as great as Elijah who would come in the power of Elijah and bear His name. Elijah understood this, God said it. However, Elijah did not die but was taken to heaven by a whirlwind, as witnessed by Elisha.

God's Spirit of prophecy ceased with Malachi, because the One whom God was sending would turn the hearts of fathers to the children, and the hearts of the children to their fathers. God's authorization was given to the One, whom He would send with an authoritative command relative to the times of vengeance upon the Jews, the desolation of the city and temple, and eventually the end of the world. This is to be understood with reverential fear in order to prevent the great and dreadful day of the Lord on the unrighteous.

God said that He would come and smite the Earth with a curse, but the people could not understand because they were not listening. They did not understand, because they refused truth and chose not to understand because of greed.

Was God silent for four hundred years?

CHAPTER 4
The Period of Silence

Nothing is spoken;
Nothing is heard;
Yet God still speaks
Deep thoughts?
Realism sets in!

IF PAST GENERATIONS COULD HAVE seen into the future, the people in the Old Testament would have seen what God had in store for them. God talked with them, took care of them, and demonstrated that He is real and alive. They could not have understood the love God now has shown for His people because of the One whom He spoke of then.

One-way communication defined the exchange; the people understood and thus acted based on what God told the prophets to tell them. God communicated what He desired of the people, and the people, some, reciprocated by their willingness to obey through faithfulness. The missing element for the people, most, was the measurement of time. Nobody is privileged to understand God's timing for His purpose.

During these four hundred years of apparent silence, empires rose and vanished, rulers emerged and died, lands were conquered, people were enslaved, and racism separated people. Societies were built, then collapsed and some were rebuilt. Jewish people came into power then fell out again and laws dictated religious practices. Men established kingdoms and built idols they worshipped as gods while compelling others to do so as well.

Faith led to unbelief, faithfulness to unfaithfulness, favor to disfavor, fellowship to estrangement, forgiveness to unforgiveness, friendship to friendlessness, and fruitfulness to unfruitfulness. Nevertheless, some remained faithful to the teachings of the prophets despite their suffering hardships and the ill effects of the ecological and environmental misfortunes of others. The faithful believers would sow wheat but reap thorns; they wore themselves out, gaining nothing. They had been God's dearly beloved, precious in His sight, but now He had given them over to their enemies. The churches blended religion with vain fashions, pursuits in greed, and pollutions as people got caught up in their follies and would not take the warnings to heart.

God took His hand off the rebellious people when they became impressed with themselves. He never closed off the power within His hand, but the ripple effect of disobedience involved others and affected them as well. The stubborn adhered to their own opinions and incorporated the opinions of others who sought after their own purposes. Those people following self-serving courses despite reason and profitable arguments, or spiritual persuasion rejected God's powerful hand. They decided that they were the measure of all things and after earnest pleas from God, God removed is hand.

As we sit in quiet meditation and try to make sense of our lives, we meet God. He meets us in our hearts, where we can feel Him. But in our noisy culture, we often act as though we detest quietness, filling our lives with any and every nerve-jangling distraction. If we want to hear God when He speaks, we must slow down, stop talking, sit quietly, and listen.

The oldest and most perfectly developed civilization of ancient times was the Egyptian empire, but it also became unstable. Egyptian monuments, relics, and customs were shaken and fell into ruins. Each dynasty was replaced by the next as behaviors and traditions became rooted in power and fashions rose, implementing diverse agendas well into the Macedonian period. The Egyptian period had great significance, positioning influential, tough people in authoritative places to shape the future. The history of Egypt seems endless, because what came after the Macedonian era and what was to take place facilitated radical transformation.

The four centuries between the Old and the New Testaments was a dark period in the history of Israel, because there was neither prophet nor inspired writer. There were scattered books and references written in Greek and Latin. From these writings, we learn that empires sprang up, others were crushed, and the Roman empire became a ruling force. During the rise and fall of empires, the Egyptians, Romans, and Caesarians wars radically shifted history through conquests and annexations, spotlighting the new world power of Rome.

Because there were no prophets or inspired writers, an Egyptian priest from Heliopolis, one of the oldest cities of ancient Egypt, began compiling Egyptian history from short transcripts and summaries done by Christian historians in previous centuries. This Egyptian priest, Manetho, conceptualized dynasties by groups, families, and other identifiers. The short transcripts and summaries put together by Christian historians in later centuries were attributed to Manetho's concepts, but they have no independent value and do not corroborate historical authenticity. Many historians reject the dating and time periods for the pharaohs as invented, but there seems to have been some connection to a political party based on exaggerating the supremacies of some of the kings and belittling others.

Manetho's concept of dynasties was cited for breaking apart kingdoms into reasonable, logical groups by locations, families, or other identifying countenances. His literary work proved to be constructive in formalizing the many groups and historical figures, giving them authoritative value in formulating the period between the Old and New Testaments.

Manetho's concepts were relevant and a critical base for the historical changes that is subjective and weighs only as hypothetical speculation. Whatever may be our approach, this critical supposition regarding the validity of the Old Testament is significant only by association. We must ask the question, how does the concept of the dynasties between the Old and New Testament period weigh in on today's structured living?

Dynasties are prevalent today, marked by socioeconomic levels dictated by religion and political structuring. When Judea became a Roman province, it was stripped of the hereditary royal power, which had been retained only by the high-priestly office. The one thing that remained was a review of the developments within the center of Judaism, which was under consideration. Most Jewish people remained loyal to the national traditions and faith, though questions remained about the condition of their spirituality and the results concerning their economy.

Remember, there were no inspired writers or prophets recording this era. God gave the writers nothing to write and the prophets nothing to teach. There was literature being written about the differences of opinion within the Jewish communities, but the literature had no canonic credibility. The old literary instinct of the nation asserted itself, for it was Jewish tradition and would not be renounced. Thus, many writings were produced according to recognized law; they weren't accepted canonically, but they still are extremely helpful for a correct understanding of the life of Israel in the dark ages between the Old Testament and Christ.

We must attempt to understand the literature of this important part of history, because it helps us understand the concept known as the *fullness of time*—the appropriate time for an event to occur in the light of specific predictive prophecy. This concept of the fullness of time follows power in words, which generate and activate faith. If you say something, it will happen in the fullness of time if you wait patiently and long enough; everything will become clear within the fullness of time.

The Intertestamental Period

The Intertestamental Period was characterized by the struggle of the Jews in Palestine to attain political and religious autonomy from a series of dominant foreign powers. The intertestamental period is the four hundred years between the testaments denoting the Jewish struggle between the end of the writing of Malachi in the Old Testament and the beginning of the events in Matthew in the New Testament. The intertestamental period is also referred to as the testament period, the essence in time between the Old and New Testament period.

Before and during the testament period, literature was produced that addressed the years of suffering, oppression, and internal strife. And because of that literature, belief was born in the inherent rights and wrongs of matters claiming respect and praise, which again influenced ruling families and groups.

In particular, three groups of writings—the Septuagint, Apocrypha, and Dead Sea Scrolls—influenced society throughout the Old Testament and well into the New Testament, and they continue to affect our beliefs today. The Septuagint became the bible of the Jews outside the Holy Land and contributed to the missionary value to prepare the world for the fullness of time. The Apocrypha describes various religious writings of the utmost importance for the correct understanding of the Jewish problem, but it is of uncertain origin; regarded by some as inspired, it is nevertheless rejected by most authorities. The Dead Sea Scrolls, found in a cave near the Dead Sea in the 1940s and containing most of the Old Testament, have been called the greatest manuscript discovery of modern times.

The fruits of the Septuagint and the Apocrypha had a profound effect on the people. The literary activity originated during the testament period, though doubtful concerning authorship and authenticity, was a turning point in spiritual history. Earlier history had been plagued by idolatry, but idolatry was slowly disappearing. Life was being supported by the abundance of surfacing literature of the times, scrupulously written but not verified, recognized, authorized, or accepted by Protestant Christians or Orthodox Jews as inspired by God. What emerged was an almost unendurable spirit of exclusiveness motivated by holiness. During the legal holiness era, profound changes occurred in response to the pressures of the intertestamental period, the struggle for religious autonomy. These pressures mounted from groups such as the Sadducees, Essenes, and Pharisees, who concentrated their beliefs on the studies of the literature that had no canonic credibility.

The Sadducees were high priests from whom the priesthood of the captives claimed descent, and they flourished in the first century. They denied the resurrection of the dead, the possibility of an afterlife, and the existence of angels and spirits. Later, historians regarded them as more of a political party of the priestly class who also rejected oral laws and traditions.

The Essenes were Palestinians who flourished from the second century, set apart by principles of asceticism, celibacy, and joint holding of property. These people followed a doctrine by which they could attain a high spiritual and moral state that would allow them to practice self-denial, self-mortification, and so on.

The Pharisees were first-century BC Jews who strictly observed religious ceremonies and practices and adhered to oral laws and traditions. The Pharisees were opposed to the Sadducees' teachings and taught from their observance of Jewish tradition as they interpreted it from writings and their learning. They believed in life after death and in the coming of the Messiah. They were distinguished by strict observances and regarded as pretentious, self-righteous, formal, and hypocritical.

Some prominent people lived during this era that birthed life into notions that opened doors to new belief systems. These new beliefs gave powers to gods that substantiated social societies and cultures that framed ways of living for so many without truth. Alexander the Great proclaimed himself a demi-god, calling himself the son of Zeus, giving himself an ordination by a divine force. Later he was told he had been a miracle child because his mother had been impregnated by the god Zeus.

Many beliefs followed from wars during the testament period. Many mighty and prominent men of the ruling dynasties articulated and ordered their interpretations of religion based upon their established laws. There were learned men who established precedence for religion by the core of self and implemented their rule upon the people. However, there were some people, namely the Jewish people, who held fast to the teachings of the Septuagint and the Apocrypha, which divided the Jewish communities.

The political, religious, and social atmosphere of the Jews changed significantly during the testament period. Great warriors fought, grouping nations into empires and fashioning dynasties. These nations were influenced directly by imposing the character of the conqueror upon the conquered people. One warrior, Alexander the Great, never forced the culture of Greece upon the dwellers of the various provinces he conquered; he merely introduced it through the Greek teaching methodology. The Greek philosopher and scientist Aristotle, Alexander's teacher, was a mentor with intent, purpose, spirit, and passion—a person who thought and admonished. Aristotle was the model for the teacher and trusted counselor for someone who's being brought up with skills, one must have to teach others.

Alexander, the student of Aristotle, was well educated in Greek philosophy and politics. Alexander required that Greek culture be promoted in every land that he conquered. Because of Alexander and others like him, empires grew, and the people succumbed to rule by force, where the ruling class altered the people's belief systems.

Motivated holiness was established, a concept brought with every emerging officialdom. But not all the dynasties had the latitude that Alexander the Great allowed to the people. He didn't force his religious beliefs upon conquered people, but he did occupy lands and require that the conquered people maintain the food supply to his troops. Unfortunately, other captured people were forced to believe whatever the ruling dynasty wanted them to, but for the Jewish people, the Greek culture was worldly, humanistic, and ungodly.

Social Developments

The social developments changed the social effects of this era and left the Jewish people without a country. Nevertheless, the learned Jewish people had established their religion not by the core of self, but by the Spirit of God through the acceptable religious writings of the inspired men of God. These exceptional people sought new ways of expressing their religion. They were cut off from temple worship, deprived of nationhood, and surrounded by pagan religious practices that threatened their faith with extinction. Now the exiled Jews turned their religious focus from what had vanished to what they had preserved.

The Septuagint and Apocrypha contained books of the Western canons that were accepted through Christian traditions, and the canon contained concepts that the Jewish people preserved. These canons are of the Old Testament and were thought to be used among the Jews combining Jewish religious traditions with elements of Greek culture during the Hellenistic period, the span of ancient Greek and Mediterranean history between the death of Alexander the Great in 323 BC and the emergence of the Roman Empire as signified by the Battle of Actium in 31 BC and the subsequent conquest of Ptolemaic Egypt the following year. The merger of the two cultures did not require the harmony of Jewish precepts or their conscience. The Septuagint and Apocrypha were the major literary products of the contact of Judaism and the Hellenistic culture. The Jewish people adopted Greek speech and ideas, and some Jewish people also adopted Greek customs but held on to their Jewish heritage.

Although the Jewish people were cut off from places of worship, they congregated in facilities they created for the purpose of worship. They were restricted from certain privileges such as carrying the Torah and literature scribed on parchment scrolls on which the Pentateuch, the first five books of the Old Testament, was recorded, which they used in their worship services. This was the new form of religious expression in the facilities that came to be known as synagogues for religious teaching and instruction. Judaism was the faith taught, and that was where the Torah could be carried. Personal devotion and building relationships with God were emphasized by means of worship services, preserving Judaism and unknowingly preparing the way for the Christian gospel.

Also, during the Old Testament period, God had transformed people by renewing their minds to become His personal servants for His will to be done in the earth realm. These men and women were considered major and minor prophets. Prophets from Moses to Malachi, whether considered major or minor, had a personal relationship with God and were sincerely dedicated to the people because of God. These men and women experienced something extraordinary that got their undivided attention and turned them to God before they met their demise. The men and women who desired the truth came out of their states of wickedness, corruption, criminality, weakness, brokenness, and unbelief to trust these believers in God.

The strong dominance of these people, mentally and physically, was brought into a place of heart-wrenching unpretentiousness sanctioned by God, that belief in Him was unquestionable, His will would be done, and His wrath was foreseeable. Notably, the prophet Jeremiah became known as the weeping prophet, for he was not afraid to cry. He wrote the book of Lamentations, a book of unabashed and unrestrained crying and mourning. He boldly declared divine judgment and refused to water down his message, preaching with fire and passion. Jeremiah was also heartbroken because God had revealed to him what was going to happen to a disobedient people—God's chosen people, the Jews.

Jeremiah's eyes were fountains of tears. He would weep day and night for his spiritually slain people, refining and testing them through his profound godly teaching because of their sin. Though Jeremiah toiled sincerely and persistently, many times reaching a conclusion, what else could he do? Still, he labored on. His message of judgment was preached through tears that flowed from a wellspring of deep compassion. God's truth was never void of love, even when His truth demanded that evildoers be judged. Jeremiah confronted the people about the time they strayed from God even though God had been faithful to them and their nation had prospered.

The people whom God had chosen to bless had deserted Him. In their sin, God told them that they had forsaken Him. They had ignored the only One who could rejuvenate and refresh them in their moments of spiritual cotton mouth. They had forsaken the spring of living water.

Thirsty? We can all identify with the human condition of being thirsty. The tongue seems to stick to the roof of the mouth, leaving barely enough saliva to swallow. We fantasize about a tall, icy glass of cold water that would satisfy our need for a drink! Water is more than a welcome relief when we are thirsty—it is necessary for life. Similarly, without the water of life, we die spiritually. Water is essential to our physical living, just as Jesus is essential to our spiritual living. In the Spirit, water symbolizes faith, salvation, and provision, and anybody who drinks the water that Jesus provides will never thirst again. That water is the Spirit of God.

Adam and Eve were separated from the Tree of Life, and thus physical death is certain. God proclaimed death for man while at the same time He provided and revealed a Savior. Continual warfare between grace and corruption still occupies the hearts of man. Jesus's death, burial, and resurrection made it possible for the Holy Spirit to come into the earth realm, and His ministry is to flow out of the heart, redeeming us back to God, the blessing to believers. The Holy Spirit supplies spiritual revelations of mercy, giving hope for forgiveness and delivering believers from the power of Satan. The term *water of life* becomes like a well springing up inside us, providing life now and in eternity. Although the body will die, the spirit lives on into eternity with or without God.

God is clear about what he expects of His people. He reiterates that He desires obedience, service, worship, loyalty, and love from us, predicated on belief. If God is so explicit, why do we have such difficulty getting it right? Jeremiah spelled out the answer: the heart is deceitful above all things and beyond cure. Jeremiah's preaching pointed to a future day when a king would fulfill all of God's covenant promises. He did not know the name of that king, nor did he know when he was coming, but he did know the person would be the righteous Branch of God. The Old Testament writers repeatedly used the word *branch* to describe the Messiah, indicating an extension of God to us and to generations to come.

Compared with the messages of the optimistic yet false prophets of his day, Jeremiah's warnings stood out like a sour note from a second-grade band student. False prophets claimed their dreams and visions were from God, but their prophecies were actually the opposite of what God had to say about the way the people were living and what they could expect as a result. God oppose them who prophesy lies in His name.

The word of God came to Jeremiah again and again concerning all the people of Judah, and Jeremiah spoke again and again, but the people did not listen. The Lord sent all His prophets to the people, but the people paid them no attention. They refused to turn from their evil ways and corrupt practices and listen to God's word.

Jeremiah's ministry was very unpopular because the prophecies were often unwelcoming. However, he ended his ministry with a ray of hope for the future. His final footnote assured that there was still hope in the guaranteeing the Messianic line to the throne of David.

The intertestamental period concerned true attitudes about readiness, stewardship, patience, charity, blameless living, perfected obedience, joyful expectations, and constant abiding. This was the time that one-way communication with God required faith. Although no prophets spoke or recorded what the Lord said, the voice of God continued to speak within the hearts of the Hasmonean family and other Jewish families who stayed faithful to God, clinging devotedly to God's promise of a messiah. These faithful people were greatly afflicted, yet they regarded with extreme repugnance the ways of the heathens, and they refused to follow the ways of the new religious sects.

The time between the testaments is referred to as the years of silence, there was no voice from God or was there?

This was a time when God did not speak because of major political and military events that sowed corruption and discord in the land. God did not speak for four hundred years, and it was a period of reflection. God was preparing to do a new thing for the Jewish people.

CHAPTER 5
Protection

The great Shepherd, Christ,
shall take care of his flock,
that the nature of troubles and
of death itself
shall be so changed
that they shall not do any real hurt.
God's people shall be delivered,
not only from evil,
but from the fear of it.

GOD PROTECTS HIS CHILDREN, THE obedient and faithful, who acknowledge His calling and worship Him. When God makes a promise, we know we can trust Him simply because at the core of His nature, He is faithful. That means He keeps His word. He is the rock, a faithful God who can do no wrong.

Each of us has been afraid, at one time or another, about something that we didn't understand. In times of fear, it is easy to forget that God is still in control and promises to rescue us. God's people, from the Old Testament times until today, have always known persecution because we live in a world where so many oppose God and His purposes. But the prophet Malachi revealed that a day is coming that will burn like a furnace, and every evildoer will be burned as rubbish.

World War II was one example of an era of persecution, but that was by no means the first time a national leader had attempted to annihilate an entire population of people. In the book of Esther, Esther played a vital role in saving the Jews, though God could have saved His people without her help. After all, He had promised that the nation would never be completely annihilated. Esther was God's handiwork. Her cousin Mordecai believed that God had allowed her marriage to the Persian king in order to stop the massacre. In the Esther story, we see clearly that God cares about His chosen people and controlled the events of that time in history.

In the book of Jeremiah, God told Jeremiah that He knew the thoughts He thought toward him, thoughts of peace and not of evil, that would give him an expected end. With these promises of God, we must focus on the commandment that God has put in front of us—to gain the promise of prosperity and the expected end, according to God's expectations for our lives. Must we hear God's audible voice during the silent periods of our lives in order to receive the benefits of the promise? What is required of us is to know that God knows all and that He is faithful and just. When righteousness flows into the heart, righteousness flows from the heart, and the mouth speaks that which flows from the heart.

We also must factor into our lives today God's promise spoken in the beginning, when He put man in the garden of Eden. God promised that if man ate from the Tree of Knowledge of Good and Evil, he would surely die. This was the promise that brought conflict between man and the serpent—Satan, the devil, who is God's enemy. The serpent was the most deceitful, shrewd, and crafty beast that God had made. With his sly demeanor, he engaged Eve in conversation and caused her to twist the truth she had been taught by Adam.

Adam had to choose between Eve (the gift) and God (the gift giver), and ignoring the consequences, he ate the fruit. Adam chose disobedience over obedience, and God kept His promise. He said that because of what Adam had done, he would return to the dust from which he had come. This meant that the promise God had made concerning eating the fruit from the Tree of Knowledge of Good and Evil would be fulfilled. People would die!

God had provided for Adam and Eve everything needed to sustain them in the garden, as well as a Tree of Life from which they could have eaten and lived forever. When Adam chose disobedience over obedience, they were thrown out of the garden and away from the Tree of Life. Yet God continued to deliver people from precarious situations, speaking through them and using them as prophets and teachers to teach the power in his word and guide people back to Him.

A thought: People were created in time, but God lives in eternity. So how long is four hundred years to God?

One of the most effective forms of deceit in Satan's arsenal is the suggestion that we can become self-sufficient. We think that we can prove our worth and achieve success in life through personal accomplishments, applying the strength of our will in skills, endurance, and ingenuity. We restrict our attention and become absorbed in that narrow path, focusing our thoughts on that particular goal, no matter where we are or who we are with. Whatever it is—a personal goal, professional objective, perceived personal slight, or a wrong to be righted—it is always on our mind.

A person can intensely focus their thoughts. Holding the focus to a goal or objective closed in the mind constricts the mind of the surroundings resulting in the loss of immediate awareness. With some people, that's all that they do purposely, knowing they are in close pursuit of their objective. Being single-minded does not mean that we lose our self-awareness or the ability to express our feelings or values, nor does it mean we are difficult to understand. It means we are able to choose to consider or ignore those things that might distract us. When we are single-minded, our minds are cool, clear, streamlined, open, and focused.

After carefully considering a certain substratum, various choices are considered and their relative objectivity are determined, the mind moves on. We feel that we are in our flow, our minds are actively being challenged, and we rise to each challenge with a mental efficiency that almost takes us by surprise. As new information arrives, we decide whether to accommodate it or discard it. Looking back, considering how we have cut a pathway through the time in life, we smile quietly to ourselves. Our confidence grows, and we are in control of what we have focused on.

However, being limited to a single thought or perspective

sometimes becomes overwhelming. We can feel that we cannot take on anything new or different regardless of the cost to us. These times become opportunities for Satan's schemes. When we are in this place of self-sufficiency, single-mindedness, we know what we're seeking, even if we do not say it aloud or whose around us, Satan is lurking.

Life is a period from an event until death. Being human is supported by life, living, and also having a spiritual experience. It is not appropriate to achieve our human goals and not our spiritual goals. We cannot be competent and a good fit for our human lives, but incompetent, inept, and a poor fit for our spiritual lives. This is a recipe for eternal spiritual damnation, which is orchestrated through the schemes of Satan.

As we go through the motions of a holy lifestyle, we can come to believe that we possess everything we need from God. We become confident in living that we feel we can take control of life from here. We learn cause and effects and have become masters over the aggressive attacks of Satan, so what can he do to us? This is what our attitudes and habits frequently proclaim. Our attitudes are shaped by the influences around us, and we become characterized by what we believe. We form behavioral habits based on stimuli and inducements, starting from birth, that appear beneficial in shaping us into adults. We learn to rationalize different stimuli and its perspectives as it pertains to our individuality, supposing the person we are.

The inducements are key factors in who we become. We are God's people, God teaches by His Word, and His Spirit helps to bring His Word into our thoughts. Therefore, our behavior is constantly being re-created, as God's Word changes us more and more into God's likeness.

In the garden of Eden, Adam and Eve encountered the serpent, who persuaded Adam to change his behavior and sin. Through Jesus's miraculous birth, leadership, death, burial, resurrection, and ascension, the Holy Spirit came into the earthly realm with infinite presence, knowledge, and guidance to help us all bring our bodies and souls into union with God.

Satan's teachings encourage us to be proud and lustful, and he talks to us contrary to the Spirit of God. Satan's inducements create spiritual warfare that causes us, without even realizing it, to fight with him. He attacks the mind and confuses the thought process. He plants variations of the truth into the psyche, but significant ineptness mars that truth. This strategy enhances our pride and causes lust to become prevalent. Again, our confidence grows, we believe that we are focused and in control of our thoughts, and we think that we can handle it. However, our decision to handle any issue on our own is contrary to God and goes against the Spirit of God which reside within us. We must realize that man is flesh, and like children, we must be taught to be like God. Man choose the nature to discern between good and evil, but if we disobey God, we die spiritually while still alive and our souls are given over to hell when we suffer the physical death. Death is not the issue here; the issue is our eternal home—heaven or damnation.

Satan engages us in warfare that we cannot win, for it is not humanly possible for us to defeat him. He is a liar and he is crafty, his father was a liar, and there is no truth in him.

One day as a turtle was swimming across a pond, he saw a scorpion on a lily pad in the midst of the pond. The scorpion yelled to the turtle, "Mr. Turtle, please give me a ride on your back to the shore. If I stay out here, I'll surely die."

The turtle looked at the scorpion and said, "No way. You are a scorpion. You'll sting me, and I will surely die."

The scorpion replied, "No, Mr. Turtle, I won't sting you. I need to get to the shore before I die."

The turtle thought about it, then asked again, "You sure you won't sting me?"

"No, I won't sting you," the scorpion replied sincerely.

The turtle swam to the lily pad, the scorpion climbed onto his back, and they swam off. Just as the turtle got to the shore and the scorpion was about to jump off, the scorpion raised his tail and stung the turtle. The turtle was shocked, and as he slowly died, he said to the scorpion, "You said you was not going to hurt me!"

The scorpion replied in a sinister voice, "You knew I was a scorpion when I got on your back."

Even today, some people are who they are because of their nature. Many influences have shaped their minds to become who and what they are, and nobody can change them. Influence is powerful, but it is useless with some people. With enough support and the power of the Holy Spirit, where wrong or right is an issue, people can and will change their thinking and behavior.

While talking with Eve, Satan twisted her thoughts about God's commandment concerning the Tree of Knowledge of Good and Evil. He persuaded her to reconsider the framework of the relationship between wisdom and the fruit, and he played down God while elevating Adam and Eve to God's level. Eve became convinced that she could touch the fruit and not die, and that her eyes would be opened regarding good and evil so that she and Adam would be like gods. Satan misled her. The knowledge of good and evil was a place Adam and Eve did not have to venture, because

God had already provided for them and with sound instruction concerning the tree.

Eve ate some of the fruit and nothing happened to her. She gave the fruit to Adam, now he was faced with the choice of obeying God or succumbing to Eve's persuasion. Should he do what Eve, his gift from God, wanted him to do by eating the fruit, or should he obey the gift giver's commandment, God, and not eat the fruit? This is the predicament Satan wants all God's people to be in, where he feeds enough chaotic information into our thought process to sway us away from God.

God commanded Adam not to eat the fruit. Adam was the keeper of the garden, and it was his responsibility to obey the commandment. Adam had the opportunity to teach Eve about God's commandment, but instead he ate the fruit. The consequence of eating the fruit was that men would die. God removed Adam and Eve from the garden of Eden because the Tree of Life was there. Adam was deemed a sinner and could not be privy to the Tree of Life; he would live as a sinner forever, and his children and their children would also be sinners privy to the Tree of Life. God told Adam on the day when Adam ate from the Tree of Knowledge of Good and Evil, he would surely die.

The consequence was twofold, for both the body and the soul, both would be separated from God. Spiritual death is of greater significance than physical death, because it separates our souls from God. Spiritual death relates to the twofold existence of man, the soul and ego where one or both being dead. The soul is our spiritual principle embodied within us, our total self, where our morals and emotions are contained. The moral forces of self – defines all rational, sentimental, spiritual, and cultural consciousness, the person's total self.

In contrast, the ego is the opinion that we have about ourselves, especially as contrasted with another self or the world. The ego, constructed in our minds, is a false part of our personality composed of both our positive and negative self-esteem beliefs. It is the part of the mind that mediates between the conscious and the unconscious, and it is responsible for reality testing and the sense of personal identity. It's the structure in our brain that gives us that person, an identity, and serves the purpose for our physical interaction with others.

We have a sinful nature that is disobedient to God. We are all born with that sinful nature, which can be traced back to Adam and Eve. Spiritual death is a state of being alienated from God and therefore lacking His life.

The Word of God teaches that there are two sources of spiritual death: the fall of man and our disobedience. Relative to the fall of man, Adam's disobedience in the garden leads us to this critical avenue, and unless we're born again, we're spiritually dead in our sins and thus lost. Spiritual death is the absence of a spiritual life. By the fall of Adam, we were cut off from the presence of the Lord and considered as dead to things temporal and spiritual. Spiritual death ensued immediately.

Disobedience brings horrible spiritual, physical, emotional, and mental consequences that separate us from God and unite us with Satan. Emotions and physical consequences related to bad things that can happen to us bring sadness and hurt, which can end tragically. The consequence that can befall us will determine where we will spend eternity.

Disobedience could lead to our own death or the death of someone close to us. We were dead in our trespasses within the sins in which we walk following the course of this world in the power of Satan who is the prince of the air. The spirit of Satan is at work in sons of disobedience among whom we have all once lived in the passions of our flesh. We carry out the desires of our bodies and the will of our minds by nature as children of violent rage and anger like the rest of humankind. And when God entrusts us to front-line spiritual warfare, disobedience carries a heavier price and the discipline of God is more severe.

People who live in self-sufficient pleasure without the Spirit of God consent to be brought to an end, such as death. Ignorant from the effects of the destructive and disruptive forces of the natural life, forbid the deeper and greater blessings that are acts of divine favor of the Holy Spirit.

It is clear that the righteous will experience spiritual death if they turn to evil, as Adam, King David, and the prodigal son did. Don't be deceived by false teachers who deny the righteous, for we all experience spiritual death. But like King David and the prodigal son, we can change our ways and come back to God, where grace and mercy abound.

Those who truly repent of their sins will not be ashamed to own their actions or fear the process of repentance. They flee to God's infinite mercy and depend upon that alone for pardoning and restoring peace. They beg for the pardon, asking earnestly and humbly through supplication. The blood of Christ sprinkled upon the conscience blots out transgressions and having been reconciled to God, reconciles us to ourselves.

We are encouraged, in our repentance, to hope that God will graciously accept us. If we deeply desire truth, we must turn from sin and dedicate ourselves to the process of correcting our lives by obedience to God's commandments according to His Word. God looks for this in a returning sinner. Where there is truth, God will give wisdom. People who sincerely endeavor to do their duty shall be taught their duty, and they will expect good only from divine grace overcoming their corrupt nature. They will be quiet and listen, slow to speak to speak the truth.

The design of death is plain. We ought to exalt our views respecting the blessings Christ has procured for us, comparing them with the evil that followed the fall of our first father, Adam. God's blessings extend not only to the removal of the evil, but beyond. Adam's sinful nature became guilt and corruption, and thus by him all have sinned. We are born into the world with a natural inclination to sin, but we're given a choice to do God's will or our own will. We naturally choose to follow our own will, despite the circumstances and challenge before us, because we think that it will profit us and satisfy our ego. When we seek to pursue our own will, we become rebellious against God.

All men experience death, like an infectious disease that none can escape—first spiritual death, then physical death unto eternal life. If Adam had not sinned, he would not have died, but a sentence of death was passed as upon a criminal. Sin prevailed for many ages before the giving of the laws by Moses, and thus death reigned a long time, not only over adults who willfully sinned, but also over multitudes of infants who knew no sin. Even children innocent of the knowledge of sin have fallen under the condemnation that the sin of Adam extended to all future generations. Adam was surety of a new covenant for all who are related to him, death would occur for his descendants and it is both spiritual and natural. The spiritual death meaning it's a permanent separation from God which is far worse than the physical death. This statement can be made about any person's earthly life, and it's repeated throughout the detailed account of Adam's descendants and remains prevalent today. God's commandment was violated, death was mandated, and so we die.

Satan is alive today and constantly deceives people as he did when he hoodwinked Eve. She didn't get the instructions from God, so her understanding may not have been clear. She may not have heard or felt the sincerity in the voice of God relating the commandment. Nevertheless, Satan chose her to make his play toward Adam. Maybe Satan would have found it more difficult to hoodwink Adam into disobeying God, or maybe he chose Eve hoping that her emotions would influence Adam's by swaying his ego. (The ego is a false part of our personality constructed in our mind. It is composed of both our positive and negative beliefs about our self-esteem.)

The natural challenge was before Adam, and the choice would profit him. Now in the consideration state, he chose to satisfy the ego. Our brain gives us our personality and identity, and it serves the purpose for our physical interaction with others. Adam's ego probably sold him on eating the fruit, rather than obeying God.

Satan twisted and embellished the truth, then aggrandized man to the woman and enfeebled God, saying the man would be equal to God. Were human emotions involved in Adam eating the forbidden fruit?

Because we allow ourselves to fall into the trap of self-reliance—"I got this all by myself"—God will allow difficulties in our lives to alert us to our need of Him. For this reason, was God silent for four hundred years? God was not silent! The power had not gone out of His Word. The Spirit of God's Word, both spoken and written, remained in the earthly realm. Apparently, God's audible voice was silent, but why?

Death is certain, but the door to spiritual progress is open. The battle between death and progress were enjoined from the very origins of the world and will continue until the last day, as God has declared. Humanity is caught in this conflict, and man is obliged to wrestle constantly with life and death if he is to cling to what is good. Man cannot maintain his own integrity without great effort and the help of God's grace, so we must change our minds concerning sin. Sin can be a matter of fact; we forgive but cannot forget. Is it that we cannot forgive or that we refuse to forgive? When God forgives sin, He remembers it no more. On our journey to becoming like Christ, we learn to forgive, forget, and move on with the expectation that prosperity is on the horizon.

Harboring unforgiveness, a tool for Satan, causes hearts to harden, and barriers established. This mindset makes it easier to believe Satan, who urges ill feelings to remain within us consciously, although inactively making us ready for destructive mental or physical actions later.

The sacred truth shall produce a spiritual change in the heart and convert the sinner. The sinner then finds peace in his conscience, and love constrains him to devote himself to the service of his Redeemer, God. The growth of God's kingdom is identified with the evolution of the world. The kingdom of God is indeed in the world and in people who live and work in the world. With the help of God's grace, man works with another in compliance together in the growth of the Kingdom of God and the fulfillment of His plan for a divine providence. God's word shall not return to Him void.

Before the New Testament, men, women, and children turned away from God and failed to keep His commandments. God gave them a gracious call through the ministry of His prophet Malachi, who taught and preached God ordinances. There was an earnest, urgent appeal to reform. God must be served in the first place, and the interest of our souls ought to be preferred before that of our bodies, including our egos.

After the Babylonian captivity, Judea was ruled by the Persians, Greeks, Egyptians, Syrians, and then the Romans, with a brief period of self-rule under the Hasmoneans. The Old Testament was translated into a Greek version called the Septuagint, which is the version most often quoted in the New Testament. Also, this period saw the rise of the Pharisees and Sadducees and an increase in the influence of the Scribes. The essentiality of the teaching by prophets is upheld miraculously by God Himself. The essence of God's Word is "Honor God first" and "Honor mankind as yourself."

Why was there silence?

> Between the time of Malachi and the coming of the Messiah, several prophecies were fulfilled, including the 2,300 days of desecration between 171 and 165 BC, but neither the fulfilled prophecies nor the 400 years the nation was given to study scripture, to seek God and to prepare for the coming Messiah, was put to good use. In fact, those years blinded and deafened the nation to the point where most of the Jews could not even consider the concept of a humble Messiah.[1]

---

[1] B.V. Johnson, *High On the Mountain*. Quoted in D. C. Collier, *My Origin, My Destiny: Christianity's Basic "Value Proposition"* (Bloomington, IN: Westbow, 2016): n.p.

Every moment of each day, the Word of God has value as a religious exercise, but for the full benefit to be received from its truths, the Word must be appropriated to personal needs.

A delivery man on a baker's wagon may handle a thousand loaves of bread per day and yet go home hungry at night. The Bible reader may peruse large portions of the Word of God with little profit; unless he makes it his own by personal appropriation and feeds upon it, he'll be hungry.

Many Christians are satisfied to receive all their truth filtered through the mind of some teachers, ministers, or commentators and seldom, or never, go to the Book of Books (the Bible) for independent study. They inevitably become more echoes of the opinions of others. They are not grounded in truth; hence they are liable to be carried about with every wind of doctrine.

Misunderstandings usually lead to minor arguments or disagreements, which have a great effect on what is believed by faith. A failure to understand causes misinterpretations that split communities into social levels predicated on power, which unfavorably settles quarreling and disagreements among people.

Many denominations of Christianity rose from different views that were fashioned during the years when there was no prophetic record of God speaking. Literature surfaced analyzing and depicting events surrounding these views, which lend vital credence to the interpretation of the intertestamental (the struggling) period. The people under strenuous difficulties in their faces ingested the literary information coupled by word of mouth propaganda formed various religious beliefs stemmed from trust or confidence. The many thoughts and feelings were derived from the readings and/or the talking and led people somewhere! Denominationalism were on the horizon, based on the thought processes depicted in the literature shaped beliefs and views. Denominations views of the literature shaped and united religious congregations and organizations who adhered to specific beliefs and practices. Much of these beliefs and practices were convoluted.

Despite the conditions some of the faithful believers found themselves in, they maintained hope in the word of God. They trusted that God would deliver them from bondage, persecution, degradation, and captivity honoring them with eternal life with Him. Although everyone succumbs to a physical death, some believers died before they saw deliverance. God has the final decision regarding whose souls are heaven bound regardless the time of death.

The intertestamental period was not a time of silence for God, but a time for people to reflect on who God is and His representation for humankind. God is all-knowing, all-powerful, and present everywhere always. God is truth, and He cannot fail. He has been useful to His worshippers, careful of them, and tender with them, and He has not changed.

God keeps us from seen and unseen danger, defends us against any alarm, rescues us from any tumble, and stands in the way of any possible threat and death. God's protective power is for us a refuge, forms a protective umbrella over us, shields us, and protects us from the cold wind of Satan. Satan is the prince of the air, a ruler who possesses no power. He manifests evil in the world through influencing people and commanding demons. The air refers to the invisible realm above the earth, the ground, where Satan and his demons move and exist.

God is certainly capable of protecting His servants. He possesses irresistible power, an unstoppable tide, power that cannot be thwarted. He's able to do anything His will directs. It is God's will to use His power to protect His people. Since God cannot lie, He will not lie, and we can have absolute confidence in His promise of protection.

Spiritually Protected

Jeremiah said the people's hearts were hard to no end, meaning there was no end to the corruption of which the human is capable. Satan had a heart problem that got him expelled from the heavens and sent to earth, so he knows about the heart and deals with the human mind to influence the heart.

Our brains set us apart from other species and we can use our rational thought processes to make decisions, consider alternatives and possibilities, and employ reasoning and calculations. God has given us the ability to choose. The mind is a battlefield where we organize conscious and unconscious mental activities that aid our ability to feel, enhance our perceptions, and challenge our thinking. Satan attacks us by rationalizing twisted concepts and truths that might seem right, and our hearts become hard because our brains are underdeveloped. We don't understand the power in God's truth and purposes, and we buy into imaginary reasoning. Our thoughts become immoral and vicious, and then our hearts turn toward that energy, and we cause suffering and distress that should be attributed to evil. We become archaic and no longer useful to God. We become objectionable, not meeting an accepted standard, notably unskillful and inefficient belonging to the early culture of creative development.

We must keep our minds truthfully active as we grow older faithfully expecting God's promises to protect us against Satan's divisive schemes. Satan's demonic spirit has been battling God since before Adam and Eve, even though he knows that he can't win. He continuously fights God using us because he knows he has no power over God but one day, in time, his time will be up. Knowing he'll never claim victory over God, he's determined to create tumultuous confusion among the people and wreck the lives of as many of us as he can before his time comes to an end.

Because Satan is a spirit, he deals in spiritual wickedness and recklessness. To understand this methodology, we must understand spiritual things. God has given man a discerning spirit, not to fight Satan, but to communicate with God by way of the Holy Spirit in prayer. Prayer is the supernatural ability, given by the Holy Spirit, to perceive the source of a spiritual manifestation of truth and the determination whether it is of God or the world.

The Holy Spirit provides knowledge and furnishes the ability to recognize and perceive spiritual awareness from God. Satan places obstacles in our path to derail our progress or cause calamity, but because of this ability given to us by the Holy Spirit, Satan's tactics fail. We're forewarned of them by the Spirit of God, and we hold fast to God's unchanging hand. When someone is targeted by Satan, they may not even realize it, especially if Satan is convincing enough to cause the person to consider taking action that will bring them misfortune. Satan is likely to bolster their pride in an effort to persuade the person to act. If the person does wrong and then is found out and punished, Satan has succeeded.

The Spirit of God, through discernment, speaks directly into a person's heart about God's position on the matter. To hear God and be receptive, the person who is granted this ability must have a relationship with God or building one. He then can decide to turn away from wickedness and turn toward God. The measure of the incident (the trap set by Satan) may not ever be revealed or known through the obedience to God by faith. By faith and understanding, spiritual manifestations are made evident in the heart first. Listening to the Spirit of God renders a capable rationale for positive decision making where real growth in spiritual maturity is realized.

Although decisions may seem uncertain and awkward regarding the facts of an issue, righteousness will prevail when the voice of God is heard through discernment. The desire to express one's feelings and emotions surfaces as a conscious impulse to act in earnest. Through discernment, the Holy Spirit implies God-like characteristics that offset the forces of the physical appetite to satisfy the emotional need of gratification.

Emotions are built in. In the conscious, mental reaction mechanisms that are subjective where strong feelings are compiled and are accompanied by physiological and behavioral changes alters the body. These changes affect feelings, excitement, and disturbances, they alter the mind to a robust and envious state of emotion. The envious outcomes may or may not seem appropriate for reasons that register within the mind regarding the targeted person. Nevertheless, follow your heart and do as God has purposed for you to do, knowing that God is working toward a favorable outcome for His glory. Just do the right thing according to what God has put into your spirit, because it's from God. It is not about you or me.

All the gifts of the Spirit of God are upon us without measure. By Christ, the Word of His gospel may bring light to those who sit in the dark, give sight to those who are blind, and grant freedom to the captive. The mandate for us is to preach the acceptable year of the Lord, because liberty is proclaimed. Declare Christ, the office of

Jesus, a wonderful name in God. In nothing is He more wonderful than in His Word, His grace, and the power that comes along with His Office. We may wonder that He should speak such words of grace to such graceless wretches as humankind, but God said that everything He created was good!

We don't know and cannot understand the difference we make or the effect of what we do for others by listening to the Spirit. The effects of our obedience is God's business, not ours. We're given resources by God to help others—our time, goods, money, and service. Whatever we are asked, in our hearts, to do or not to do, we should obey as unto the Lord.

Satan is here to steal from us and kill us. He will seek to destroy any creation of God. He has always been a liar whose purpose is to bring death and destroy what God puts into our hearts. Satan is the author of grief, brokenness, sickness, spiritual death, and physical death, and he will spare nobody—young or old, black or white, sick or healthy, male or female, poor or rich.

We should be more concerned for other people than for ourselves. What we do directly or indirectly affects others. Whether or not we know a person, our disobedience to God could be a catastrophe for another, either now or in the future. We cannot know what will happen in the future, the mystery should propel us to watch and pray for the truth of the living God by the help of the Holy Spirit.

God's love, faithfulness, and protection are for everyone regardless of creed, color, ethnicity, or economic status. God sees our hearts and does not force anything on us but gives us the choice of following the path He has laid out or not. God is spiritually beside us to guide us if we accept Him into our hearts and employ Him to turn us from our wicked ways and acknowledge Jesus as the Messiah.

All we must do is ask whatever it is we desire of our God in Jesus's name for help and make it our business to follow His instructions. The Holy Spirit will intervene in our lives and direct souls back to God. Therefore, we must establish a personal relationship with God through studying the Bible, understanding the Word for His purposes, and spiritually obeying His will for our lives. We must allow Jesus to reign in our hearts so that we can hear and obey by faith, the Holy Spirit.

God foresaw the problems that the pastor would face if he was offered the job for which he had applied. God knew the pastor's heart was focused on helping bring people back to Him. The new job would cause problems for his ministry and service to God, creating stress and complicating the pastor's life. God works for the good of those who love Him and those who have been called according to God's purpose. The pastor didn't know what the future held for him concerning this job, but the position would have had grave consequences for people attached to his ministry.

God revealed Himself to apostle Paul. The revelation was so dramatic Apostle Paul's learning was so compelling he wrote the majority of the New Testament. Apostle Paul taught the Romans and because God said it He made it enjoyable. The road to Christianity may be rocky, seemingly unfair, and uneven in life, still it is an enjoyable journey.

The peace of God guarded the pastor's heart, and the pastor was thankful that he didn't get the job. In his opening prayer, although he had no idea what was taking place, he thanked God, being careful because of the unknown. But when he found out what the job entailed; he was overwhelmed with awe that God delivered him from the scheme of captivity Satan had set. The pastor gave thanks to God again this time with a deeper sincerity glorifying God with thanksgiving for the protection from Satan's scheme of destruction.

In the lives of many believers, there are idle periods when God seems strangely silent. Perhaps that's never been truer than during the four centuries between the end of the Old Testament and the beginning of the New. Malachi was the last of the Old Testament prophets, and after his death, God did not send a successor until the birth of John the Baptist.

It isn't difficult to visualize the Old Testament prophets, whose primary role was not to pronounce doom and gloom on God's unfaithful people but to proclaim the coming of the Savior. Malachi closed his prophecy with words that should have infused all future generations with hope. Surely the day was coming, he said, when people would see God's righteousness, and there would be healing for God's people when Elijah appeared. The Elijah of whom Malachi spoke of would be the John the Baptist, whose mission would be to prepare the people for the ministry of the One who would set them free from slavery and death of sin.

People in spiritual captivity are spiritual prisoners of war. They are darkened in their understanding of spiritual things including their own conditions. When a person is in spiritual captive, they will lose their sense of purpose or aspects of it and is at the disposal to their masters. A spiritual slave in captivity has no right to choose his path in life or even his daily routine. The master, Satan, calls the shots for his slaves but the promised One would set them free from his captivity. The slave master Satan control the reins to sin and death.

The One, Jesus Christ, has power over Satan that Satan can

no longer wield the stranglehold of sin and death he once did. The stranglehold of selfishness, greed, and lust now broken and allows us to offer ourselves as willing participants of the Lord Jesus Christ. Death is the result of sin made manifested by the laws established in the Old Testament. Being set free from the laws of the Old Testament which covered sin, means the establishment of the new and better covenant not just covered sin and death but erased from existence, leaving no historical fingerprint of the sin ever happening. Without sin, there could be no spiritual death and if a sin was committed, God would forgive that sin and it would be as if the sin was never committed.

When we are in Christ Jesus, we are free. Christ Jesus is like a strong fortress that Satan cannot penetrate. When we walk in the Spirit of God, praying, and worshipping then we experience that the law of sin and death just glance off us.

But slavery, sin, and death came as the result of captivity of men controlling other men. People wants and needs for their fleshly desires flourished which led to the institutionalizing of our minds to the greed of laurels instead of seeking God; designs useful to Satan. Satan maybe powerless to God but he's crafty enough to trick God's people.

Today it seems we are unable to contact our Lord. We inevitably experience the same fears and doubts that the Old Testament generations felt. Living during times of apparent one-way communication requires faith and obedience. Was God silent during the intertestamental period, or was His Word relevant and doing what it was meant to do? Even though there had been no prophet since Malachi, the people had already received God's promises, they had access to the recorded Word of the Lord. The faith of some, no doubt, matured during that one-way communication vacuum.

They continued to turn to God in faithfulness while clinging to His promises of hope.

What life must have been like during the intertestamental period struggling in time with no divinely inspired prophets, no message from God—only a seemingly endless void. Some people likely assumed that God had forgotten them. Others may have concluded that He no longer cared. We've all experienced one-way communications and felt doubt at one time or another on different subject matters. But without faith, it's impossible to please God, so blind faith and authentic worship mean relying on God based on His promises and our obedience solely.

Concepts in the Bible that were true yesterday are still true today. Faith without works but works without faith are just as dead. Faith is the substance of things we hope for and the evidence of things we can't see. In other words, if God said it, we're supposed to believe it, because belief advances God's purpose. We don't know what tomorrow holds, so we must trust God's infinite knowledge that whatever we're doing within God's will works for the good of those who love the Lord and are call together for God's good. The Word of God speaks, whether or not we hear it.

There was a deacon who weighed 375 pounds and had a severe case of diabetes. One afternoon while driving home from church, he passed a doughnut shop and decided to stop. The parking lot was full, and the line at the drive-through window was extremely long. So the deacon circled the parking lot, hoping that someone would leave or, better yet, that the drive-through line would diminish. Unfortunately vehicles in front of him were pulling into parking slots as quickly as they emptied, and while he waited for a parking slot, additional cars kept entering the drive-through line. As he continued to drive around the lot, suddenly a parking slot became available. He parked his car, went inside, bought some doughnuts, and enjoyed them on the way home.

The same evening, the man's sugar count exceeded the safe level, and he got very sick. He prayed to God, "Why didn't you stop me from getting those doughnuts?" But if the deacon had paid attention to the signs concerning his desire for the doughnuts, he wouldn't have gotten sick—at least not from the doughnuts. He had rationalized his erratic behavior until he acquired the doughnuts.

What message had he received from Satan that had fed his ego and caused him to ignore God's word radiating in his heart? If we listen to the Holy Spirit and carefully consider the messages that God causes our heart to send to our brain, we will dispel the ego.

The deacon had searched for something that was not available to him, but his determination to find a parking slot had closed the path between his heart and his brain. His tenacity had cost him time and gasoline, and the doughnuts could have sent him into a diabetic coma and possibly caused his death. He should have heeded the message that the doughnuts were not available to him and gone home. Grace and mercy had availed him much in the face of disobedience; God protected him from physical death. But to save himself from spiritual death, the deacon needed to repent asking God for forgiveness to return to God.

Instead of repeatedly circling the parking lot, he should have left. Being eager to find a parking slot had heightened his desire for a doughnut, and then he ended up buying several. Meanwhile Satan was playing reveille, a signal to get up in the morning, because he was trapping somebody. Soon the day will set, and he'll play taps, the last bugle call at night blown as a signal that lights are to be put out. Satan used the deacon's health issues and his desires to destroy him by meddling in his mind.

The call of scripture is always urgent with every beat of our heart saying, "Today!" The deacon knew that he had a sugar problem and that doughnuts could and would elevate his sugar count. What made him so determined to satisfy his desire for a doughnut? The parking lot had been full of cars and there was nowhere to park. The drive-through line was unusually long, so the wait would have been agonizing long. The best outcome would have been for the deacon to go home so that his sugar count wouldn't become elevated.

The deacon's desire for doughnuts, especially when he knew what the consequence would be, suggests a mental illness. The physical illness resulted from his mental illness, the elevated sugar count and the spiritual death resulted from his decision not to adhere to the proper course of action as suggested by God. The physical death would have been the result of the imbalance of the sugar count. The deacon's decisions and actions were disruptive and damaging, both spiritually and physically. Where did the confrontation come from? If not God, then Satan. Life is short, death is sure, time is passing, and the lost of the living will perish into eternity.

There is an urgency for all people. Some people voices speaking today will be silent a year from now and will speak no more. Life is like driving in the same direction on a three-lane freeway, with cars in all lanes. Some cars are carefully changing lanes preparing to leave the freeway before reaching their exit. The reality is we're all going to exit the freeway at some point. Does it make sense to drive in the outer two fast lanes until the very last minute and then hurriedly cross several lanes of traffic to avoid missing your exit?

A prepared driver knows where he's going, and prepares to exit before he gets there. How much sense does it make to develop in the knowledge of obedience before we get to our transitioning door? When we exit the freeway of life, it's eternal; we go through the doorway either to eternal heaven or eternal hell.

Our minds can lead us to the wrong place so that we get stuck in the outer lanes. When death occurs, we stand in judgment with no positive contributions to the will of God. The wisdom of knowledge is dangerous in the sense that it requires a righteous heart. A little bit of wisdom is just not enough. We must become mentally educated with God's wisdom and understanding as we travel through life, so that when we get to our exit, we go to an eternal home with God.

Traveling across lanes on the freeway endangers others. We don't know the mental or physical state of another person, but God does. Our plight for obedience on the freeway of life might save another person's life, spiritually or physically, or serve some other purpose of God's choosing.

The prophets of the Old Testament often spoke of their messages as a burden from the Lord. Perhaps it was the gravity of their words and the weight of delivering them to people who didn't want to hear, or perhaps the people didn't want to accept accurate, real-life representation without idealization of those messages. The people did not embrace the effects of heredity and the environment upon human life nor character development. Nevertheless, the Lord sustained the Old Testament people with prophets delivering God's word, and today He sustains us by the presence of the Holy Spirit, helping us to develop a hereditary character that's environmentally useful to all.

God speaks to us through His providence. The word of God came to the prophet Jeremiah, saying, "Before I formed thee in the belly I knew thee; and before thou camest forth out of the womb I sanctified thee; and I ordained thee a prophet unto the nations." (Jeremiah 1:5)

How did God speak to Jeremiah? Jeremiah does not tell us. Was it important that God spoke to him or what God said to him? The importance was what God said also what God did for him and others alike.

God speaks to His chosen ones in a variety of ways. He spoke to Moses through an angel's voice from a burning bush and He also spoke to Gideon through an angel. He spoke to Isaiah through a national crisis: "In the year king Uzziah died," he heard the voice of the Lord. God spoke to Simon Peter through a vision, and He spoke to Samuel in a whisper. He spoke to the apostle Paul through a blinding light and a booming voice.

God spoke to me in the recesses of my heart. I felt a heavy feeling one morning in Arkansas while I stood looking over the lake. A cool breeze blew off the lake and sent chills throughout my body at the same time a calmness came over me. I felt my psyche stirring, but my heart weighed in and my voice answered, "Yes, I'll preach your word." Ever since that morning by the lake, the Spirit of God has counseled me. I had to learn to distinguish between listening to my heart and my brain. I began studying the Word of God whereby I'm learning God's character. It's not hard to follow the Spirit when He's speaking to me, but the challenge is sometimes accepting the truth. But I realize this battle with Satan is between Satan and God; more than often, the Holy Spirit wins.

I don't know how God speaks to you, but I know He will. God knows what He's doing, and He'll do it regardless of how we feel. Don't try to hold God to one method of communication. God is at least as smart as we all are. He knew it would only take a whisper to get young Samuel's attention, just as He knew it would take a booming voice and a blinding light to reach the hardened Apostle Paul. God knew what it would take to get the Old Testament people's attention, as he spoke through the prophets before Malachi.

There was undoubtedly a sickness among the people of the Old Testament concerning their spirits and souls. Corrupt behavior plagued the people everywhere and was especially prevalent among God's chosen people. Because the sickness was spiritual, the remedy had to be religious, and while the solution was available, only a few people took advantage of it. If healing is to take place, the sick must adhere to the healer's commandment and choose to be healed. God is the healer, told His people that they could rejoice in Him as their light toward all afflictions. He told them whoever beholds true faith will find their godly delight enlarged, their hatred of sin increased, their souls made more watchful, and their lives more holy.

God's words are addressed not just to unbelievers and evildoers, but to the entire world: believers also. We are all God's people. Some of us are separated from God by unbelief and sin, however for as long as we're alive, we have the opportunity to return to God. If we die before being reconciled to God, then we have chosen to spend eternity in damnation. What held the Old Testament people back was not the strength of the enemy, but the lust of the people and the weakness of the church to convert people by renewing their minds.

It only takes a few people to make a difference. Sodom and Gomorrah perished for the lack of ten righteous men. A few people can make a difference in any church, school, or community. With the help of the Holy Spirit, we can do all things through Christ, who strengthens us at the asking. Therefore, we build our most holy faith and become like God as an example of His power, grace, and mercy.

No virtue is more complicated than humility, and nothing dies harder than pride and self-sufficiency. The most significant "ism" confronting the church today is not liberalism, materialism, hedonism, or fundamentalism—it's egoism. People must humble themselves before God, and He will lift us and bless us. If we are busy building the kingdom of Susan or Randy or Bill instead of the kingdom of God, He will not bless us. Don't get grace and mercy confused with blessings. Grace is unmerited, and God hands out grace because He chooses to and gives it to whomever He wants. Mercies are acts of divine favor of God's compassion and kindness which is given to us because of God's love. Grace and mercy cannot be earned, they are freely given to us. Blessings are associated with our protection and happiness. God's blessings are meant to protect us, guide us to the path of righteousness, and give us hope.

We are taught and many people believe that God's gifts rest on shelves, one shelf above the other. The taller we grow in Christian character, the more quickly we can reach more gracious and beneficial gifts. The truth is that God's gifts rest on shelves one beneath the other and it's not a question of growing taller but stooping lower. The lower we go in humility, the more of God's rewards we find. Giving our physical life for God's purpose is the ultimate sacrifice. Still, a heavenly eternal home where peace is and wearing a crown of experience in the company of Christ, is a far more significant accomplishment for the soul. But during the Old Testament period leading up to the New, non-believers, the Pharisees, and Sadducees gained momentum where the development of history corresponded to the feeble beliefs which were manufactured. These beliefs were manufactured out of the righteousness of egoism which had inflated the mines of the people including God's people. Because egoism causes people to reach for higher plateaus, they appear to be becoming better, greater, and stronger but egoism tarnishes hope - hope drifts into hopelessness, and the certainty of physical death predestines the soul to eternal damnation.

Prayer is the secret of a progressive spiritual life. It is the secret not only to a great experience but to a great church as well. We must not forget that God is spirit and truth. By His Spirit He created male and female. He spoke of the triune: "Let us ..." He later created physical bodies and blew His breath of life into the man, who became a living soul. The woman was made of the stock from which Adam was created with the Spirit of God already inside of her. In the spirit, God spiritually gave them dominion over all the earth. Where was Satan? Satan was on the earth; therefore, we have dominion over him too. Our prayers supersede any and all powers in the will of God through belief and faith towards the greatness in life.

Man and woman are created flesh and blood and have spiritual dominion over the earth. We are mental beings with physical experiences, and we need help fighting Satan, who is spirit. We need the Spirit of God working inside us, helping us maintain our dominion over the earth by defeating Satan's schemes while on our spiritual journey toward eternity. Remember, after the sixth day of creation, God finished His work knowing that all things were complete. God reigns over the entire universe, and He is all powerful and forever present to everyone. His Spirit is available to us. God said what needed to be said to us and for us to get attached to Him. He need not to repeat the same things to us and keep getting the same results. We may not hear the audible voice of the prophets such as in the Old Testament era or during the four hundred years – the silence, rest assured God has not given up on us.

Communication with God will never be a one-way conversation. God already knows what we need, but as children, we must ask for it. He will determine the value of our request—whether it will protect us from spiritual or physical death, and/or whether it will solidify or hinder His purpose. Conversations with God must take place. We exchange information with God through prayer, signs, and behavior—our pathways to His blessings and to His unmerited grace and mercies. People and churches must rise to God's mandate, to realize through prayer that our achievements are accomplished in God's strength. To operate in God's power, first we should get on our knees, reverencing Him and sincerely acknowledging Him in prayer as our, Heavenly Father.

God has no obligation to answer the prayers of unbelievers, but He may. There are other reasons why God may not answer prayers, our misunderstanding of God's priorities, and our circumstances might have to change before God answer the prayer (this delay maybe to see how serious we are willing to pray). God's desire to give us more than the simple answer to our prayers making the answer once it is received, all the sweeter.

The main problem with our prayers is that we don't pray earnestly and within God's will for us. We ought to pray according to God's teaching with sincerity. We ought to pray asking for God's strength to accomplish what we need in order to advance His kingdom. We must pray without ceasing for God's will to be done for us over our lives while growing spiritual. We grow spiritually when we understand that we don't need to understand why or what God is doing, we need to be obedient that whatever He command of us,

God is advancing His kingdom. God chose all of us as His people, but not everyone has accepted Him as their Lord. Some people elect not to follow God for whatever reasons, but they pray.

God still showers people with grace and mercy. He gives grace and mercy to all of us because He loves all us and makes no distinctions among us. Yet He speaks to all people, but He obligated Himself to answer prayers of the people who are called by His name. These people earnestly seek Him in search of His righteousness, and when they find Him, they humble themselves then pray. They pray according to His will seeking His spiritual strength.

We need the power of the Spirit to accomplish the goal of advancing God's kingdom. We must seek God through fellowship in obedience, worship, and reverence in love with allegiance to His deity. Our prayers must be expressed in humility and devotion, our pathways to God's heart.

We must delight in our search desiring to learn of God. If our desire is from our hearts, God said He will give us the desires of our hearts. Our hearts must be filled with the learned qualities of love as expressed by God and explicitly carried out in our daily walk reaching the hearts of others. We will begin building our most holy faith as we discover the intimacy of God searching and putting on newfound behaviors. From seeking God comes knowledge of Him, and from experience comes the wisdom of His word. Then comes God's power, His strength of the word to speak those things that be not as though they were, God will work on behave of His methodology of love in His timing to fulfill His purpose.

We cannot expect the outcome of our prayers to be exactly what we prayed for, because it is God's plan, purpose, and result. How could we know what we don't know?

Study to Learn!

Moses talked to Aaron about speaking. Aaron was very observant of what God said to him through Moses, and he conveyed that which God gave Moses to the people. Now God does Aaron the honor of speaking for Him, because Aaron's embodiment of God's Spirit offers approval for the principles of right and wrong in behavior.

God spoke concerning clean and unclean things. One of His commandments was that teachers should not go into the tabernacle after consuming wine; teachers must not fail to discharge the duties of their office because of being intoxicated. Teachers might be able to distinguish between that which is sacred and that which is familiar, and they may never confound the two. But the concern is that God's ministers are to differentiate between clean and unclean things and people, holy and unholy things, and people. Teachers may be able to separate the precious and the vile, and ministers might be able to teach truth. Teaching was part of the priests' work, and those who were addicted to drunkenness were unfit to teach God statutes.

Nevertheless, some priests in their drunkenness taught practical truth, though they were deprived of spirituality. Students become spiritually aware of the Holy Spirit's absence and interpret the external person as Satan. Those who live after the flesh can have no experimental acquaintance with things of the Spirit. Such teachers tear down with one hand what they have built up with the other.

God set an office for priests to minister His unadulterated Word. They were supposed to earn the office, abide by it, and then teach the principal substance with compassion, helping those who are sick, hungry, or in trouble. God will use an extraordinary event to create a profound experience that He and only He will be accredited for the favorable result which confounds intelligent minds. The truth in the testimony will incorporate crazed and exaggerated praise that is transient and filled with enthusiasm.

Old Testament teachings proclaimed women to be unclean if they had issues with their menstrual cycle or continued bleeding after giving birth. The abnormal bleeding rendered them socially damaged, although through no fault of their own. Scripture relates that the blood issue affected not only the woman but their households, husbands, and communities as well. Let us not concern ourselves that the scriptures came from God.

But was the defamation the women suffered warranted?

Abnormal menstrual cycles and vaginal damage were uncontrollable issues that pertain solely to women. God described the methodology for their cleanliness in the scriptures. Women were responsible for keeping their bodies cleansed of blood issues. But women were under critical scrutiny and made to endure embarrassment, abuse, alienation, and mistreatment because of a lack of understanding of the scripture, which fueled emotions and untruths.

Anyone who touched anything that a woman had sat upon had to wash their clothes and bathe themselves, and they would be considered unclean until they adhered to the religious law and social customs outlined by the Bible. If blood was on a woman's bed or anything that she had sat upon, and another person touched it, that person was considered unclean until they had performed the cleansing ritual. If a man lay with a woman who was bleeding and her blood got on him, he and the bed would both be considered unclean for seven days. If a woman continued to bleed for many days, she would continue to be deemed unclean. Every bed she lay or sat upon would be unclean. Anyone who touched those things would be unclean until they washed their clothes and bathed. If a woman stopped bleeding, she would be deemed clean after seven days.

We need not concern ourselves with the fear of blood contamination, but with the sin. We do not need burdensome ceremonial purifications, because God sees and knows all things. He is even aware of things that escape people's notice. It is not clear how many man-made concepts of uncleanliness that have plagued emotions, which has contributed to the analogy of the issue of blood. Like other detailed entities, what God named in His statutes as unclean could be called by any of these names: infected, unhygienic, unsanitary, impure, and so on.

A rule of conduct was established by man and embedded in the people's psyche; then it was enforced with the threat of being stoned to death. The conduct man had set outside scriptural stature was demeaning and deadly. Women bore the brunt of criticism and ridicule when their bodies naturally separated tissue within their wombs and discharged it through the vagina with blood or after giving birth. Many times, biological issues prevented their bodies from ceasing to bleed.

God used the issue with blood and miraculously healed a woman who had been suffering for twelve long years. Men and women alike had been swindling her wealth while promising a cure. She believed if she could touch the hem of Jesus's garment, she would be made whole. By faith, she touched Jesus's garment, and power was transferred from Jesus to her and her blood issued was healed. Jesus told her that her faith had made her whole. Not cured, but whole! She was fully restored, with nothing missing or broken, and she regained her wealth and everything she had lost through deceit.

Seeking God through perseverance, reverent love, allegiance, and humble devotion is our pathway to His blessings. Nevertheless, being considered unclean because of bleeding should not reflect badly on a woman's character, should Satan try to destroy her soul with sin. Now think about Satan having wide and general destruction accessibility to the people who morally and practically defamed women over issues they had no control over.

A pastor had been part of a revival, and he yearned in his heart for God to do something in his life and for the church that could not be explained by an organization or through manipulation. One night the Holy Spirit came over the service with a profound conviction of power. Nothing new or unusual had happened, except that the congregation was truly worshipping in truth while genuinely seeking God. There was an original conviction in the hearts of the people. New commitments were made, and unsaved people were drawn to God in the church. It became evident to everyone who were there that night that the Holy Spirit was present in a unique way.

Yes, something was different. It was the same congregation worshipping, the same pastor preaching, and the same choir singing. The difference was the sincerity in the worship. Worshipping God means seeking His face, just as scripture described Joseph trying to find his brothers in the field. Similarly, Pharaoh tried to find Moses, who was a fugitive from justice after killing the Egyptian soldier, and Saul tried to find his lost animals. That's how we are to seek God. In doing so, we learn to operate within God's will, implementing His principles and precepts for His purposes, which makes us beneficiaries of His promises which protects us as we get close to Him.

CHAPTER 6

The Second Adam

The last Adam was
made to make and keep alive,
and supply His
Holy Spirit
to the souls of humanity.

Adam became a sinner and was sentenced to death
before he became the leader of a family. Christ bore

sin, and died to it, while leading those who believed. Till He died, He abode alone, after death, He had much fruit. And as there never was a hope for man in another, so none other can rival Him. He is the last Adam, no less than the second man.

—William Kelly

WHEN GOD SAID, "LET US," the word *us* denoted the Trinity— the Father, Son, and Holy Spirit. *Godhead* is a word used to express the doctrine of God's co-existence as three distinct persons. God spoke creation, male and female, into existence in His image with all elements of Himself: God the Father, Son, and Spirit. Then He created the physical bodies—first of Adam, the man, and then of Eve, the woman. The character of God needs to be developed within these bodies.

After sin was committed in the garden of Eden, God enforced consequences and cursed the ground. The crowning result for violating God's commandment is death. Then Adam and Eve were sent from the garden, and their access to the Tree of Life was revoked, ensuring their physical end. The essence of Adam being sent away from the Tree of Life is he was made from the dirt and after his death, his body would return to the earth.

The consequences levied upon Eve were equally profound. God said, "I will greatly multiply thy sorrow and thy conception; in sorrow, thou shalt bring forth children; and thy desire shall be to thy husband, and he shall rule over thee." Genesis 3:16

The word *Adam* means "man," and *Eve* means "living" or "mother of life." Adam and Eve are the parents of the entire human race. The first man and woman were intelligent and creative, and God designed them with the abilities necessary to rule as He had intended. They could talk with God and with each other in fellowship that was not corrupt in any way. Eve was designed to be Adam's helpmeet, suitable for him without any narrow qualifications, prescribed limits, or cultural restrictions. It was not specified how she was to express and apply her help towards Adam. Adam was commanded by God not to eat the fruit from the tree of the knowledge of good and evil before Eve was made. She lacked the matter of importance of the command of eating from the forbidden tree, nevertheless, still dangerous. For her the commandment not to eat the fruit of the forbidden tree required much thought and consideration in the understanding. But Adam chose not to educate her and excepted her analogy concerning the forbidden fruit choosing to turn from God plunging into sin and taking with him all humanity. Though not entirely, we all were marred by sin, but God put a redemption package in place.

God instituted powerful feelings of ill will for Satan, and intense dislike was levied against him. God proclaimed war between the seed of the woman and the seed of the serpent, and the woman's seed was destined to destroy and ruin the snake. The great redeemer would break his head, and the fruit of this enmity is the continual warfare between grace and corruption in the hearts of God's people.

God served the serpent notice that the redeemer was coming. The redeemer's incarnation was coming in the flesh. His coming in the seed of a woman was a great encouragement to sinners. Christ's suffering and death points at Satan bruising his heel on Christ's human nature. Christ's suffering would continue in the suffering of God's people through temptation, persecution, and death, which bruises the heel of Christ. However, while the heel is bruised on earth, the head is in heaven, and as the gospel gains ground, Satan falls.

The topmost glory of everything God created is humanity. Before conception and while in the womb, we are granted His mercy and grace, secured to an expected end with promised blessings. These blessings are predicated on obedience to God in defeating Satan.

God gave us a constitution that develops as we journey through time, strengthening our makeup, especially our health, strength, and appearance of our bodies. The Old Testament people hastened toward old age without entreating God, while calamities and irregularities confused some, leaving others feeling abandoned. But God did not cast them far off or fail them when their strength seemed to fail. God carried them in everlasting arms laid under them in Moses's time. God graciously engages to support and comfort His servants, even into their old age until their physical death.

When we begin to grow weary and unfit for business, God reminds us He is who He say He is. He is the very same God who protected us while carried in the belly and birth through the womb. People change, but God is the same. He is the Lord, and the Lord changes not, for there is none like Him.

A New and Better Covenant

The Ten Commandments were part of the Mosaic law and formed the covenant between the Israelites and God. The law eventually included more than six hundred additional man-made and initiated commandments. The original agreement included God's promise that He would take care of the people of Israel and they would prosper if they obeyed the Mosaic law.

The time has come when covenants will be renewed, expanded, and applied in a radically new way. The renewed agreement for the future upholds the promises made throughout the Old Testament period. The most significant change to the new and better covenant will regard the covenant's administrator, for this will no longer be a Mosaic covenant under God's direction. Moses brought the Israelites out of Egypt and led them through the parted Red Sea and the Sinai Desert, where they were given the original covenant. The covenant spoke to those under the law, for they are accountable to God. No human being will be justified in God's sight, since through the law comes knowledge of sin.

A large part of the Mosaic covenant was the Ten Commandments, the reason the Mosaic covenant was called the law. With the covenant came God's promises

- to make the Hebrew people His chosen people among all nations if they keep His commandments,
- to make the people of Israel a holy nation and a kingdom of priesthood, and
- to give them the Sabbath as a day of rest and tell them to keep it holy.

These commandments were, without a doubt, violated. No one could keep the commandments because of people's sinful nature. We're all imperfect.

No one could declare righteousness in God's sight by observing the law; instead, through the law they became conscious of sin. Without the law, they couldn't be aware of what God deems as wicked. The law called for love and faithfulness, with obedience and faith being the basis for the law. The law spelled out ways the

Israelites would live if they genuinely felt their future was secure in God. The law pointed to the need for a savior. Failing to keep the covenant paved the way for God's new covenant, which would become the only way to reconcile with God.

God established a covenant with King David, framed as the Davidic agreement. This covenant promised David and Israel that the Messiah (Jesus Christ) would come from the lineage of David and the tribe of Judah, and that Messiah would establish [the] kingdom of God. Then God promised that David's son, Solomon, would succeed as king of Israel and build God a temple. As the promise was being revealed, it began turning into something different: the promise of an everlasting kingdom that would endure forever. Solomon would build a physical house for God's name, but also in the promise, another Son of David would rule forever and build a lasting spiritual house.

The Davidic covenant was unconditional; God placed no conditions of obedience upon its fulfillment. The surety of the promise rested solely on God's faithfulness and did not depend on David or Israel's willingness. God provided a place for His people, the Israelites, and would plant them there so that they could have a home of their own and no longer be disturbed. The wicked people would no longer oppress them.

The promise that David's *house, kingdom,* and *throne* would be established *forever* is significant, because it showed that the Messiah would come from the lineage of David and create a kingdom from which He would reign. The covenant is summarized by the words *house,* promising a dynasty in the lineage of David; *kingdom,* referring to a people who are governed by a king; *throne,* emphasizing the authority of the king's rule; and *forever,* emphasizing the eternal and unconditional nature of this promise to David and Israel.

The reason the Davidic covenant is relevant for twentieth-century Gentiles is that God's mandate included not just the responsibility to establish a righteous ruler in Israel forever, but also to put that ruler over the church and then over all the world. When God has completely fulfilled all the promises of the Davidic covenant, the house of David will be planet Earth.

The great prophet Isaiah saw the glory of the Son of David more clearly than anyone and virtually identified Him as God.

Isaiah said, "For unto us a child is born, unto us a son is given: and the government shall be upon his shoulder: and his name shall be called Wonderful, Counsellor, The mighty God, The everlasting Father, The Prince of Peace. Of the increase of *his* government and peace *there shall be* no end, upon the throne of David, and upon his kingdom, to order it, and to establish it with judgment and with justice from henceforth even for ever. (Isaiah 9:6, 7)

The surety of the covenant with David lies ultimately in the fact that God Himself will come as King and sit upon that throne. When an agreement is conditional and also guaranteed, you can be sure that God Himself will intervene to fulfill the conditions.

Jesus Christ had been typified by the Old Testament mediators as to who would be the mediators of the new and better covenant. Jesus will inaugurate, fulfill, and permanently establish the renewed covenant that Jeremiah prophesied. The renewed covenant will initiate the entire New Testament era, cover it entirely, and reach into the eternal reign of Christ and the Father. The Messiah would emerge from the Jewish faith from within the lineage of David as the scripture had said, and the woman who would carry the child to birth would be a Jewish virgin. The seed would be of God: pure, holy, and blameless. At long last, God unveiled His Son, thus accomplishing His eternal purpose for His people. It is through Jesus that we may approach God with freedom and confidence.

With Jesus being the focus of our lives in whom we can place our trust, we can approach the Father with assurance and with confidence. Jesus is the administrator of the new, better covenant and the only mediator we need to contact the Father. His death, burial, and resurrection have bridged the gap between God and us. Our prayers are more than one-sided conversations; through prayer, we have the power to transform our lives as we are drawn nearer to our loving Lord in obedience. Drawing nearer to God through Lord Jesus is the developmental process by which we approach a spiritual likeness to God, which is almost incomprehensible.

Those who believe Jesus is Lord are making way for peace and reconciliation between themselves and their sinful nature. They are lovers of peace on earth, especially in God's churches where believers gather to get instructions on how to improve their moral and religious knowledge. Jesus's peace conveys to believers a way of making two different ideas coexist. Jesus creates spiritual peace in the hearts and consciences of His people; therefore, we must, according to our power, give to the necessities of the souls and bodies of men. People must search the scriptures, and as ministers teach according to biblical authoritatively imposes. The recipients of the teachings ought to receive their instructions as the word from God not the teachers.

Scripture identifies God as having brought Jesus through the early attempt on His life by King Herod, who wanted to have Jesus killed after birth to His death, burial, and resurrection. Jesus suffered degradation and humiliation, betrayals to arrests. He was lied on, talked about, and mistreated. He was beaten, whipped, made to drag a heavy wooden cross all the while shedding of His blood. The blood Jesus shed was for us an everlasting covenant with Him becoming the administrator and to sit at the right hand of the Father. Jesus has all the essential elements of the Godhead, and He possessed all the vital aspects of human nature—a human body, soul, mind, will, and emotions.

Jesus experienced how human qualities and emotions arise from human experiences. Being human, Jesus could and did fully understand human emotions. Humanity enabled Jesus to regain man's lost dominion and bring many sons to glory. He empowered humans to serve a sympathetic High Priest to disarm Satan, deliver God's people from the fear of death, by purchasing salvation for all by shedding His blood. Becoming flesh was a conscious choice on God's part for His Son to become that Godman, a second Adam from heaven, to save lost souls. As a result, Christ Jesus became the author and perfecter of our faith. Jesus had to be genuinely God so that He could satisfy God's wrath, a response to evil, and secure for us true righteousness and life.

We progressively develop skills through Jesus by faith and obedience, taking steps toward growth, diligence, and patience while studying our way into maturity. Following Jesus's practices of good works solidifies mental growth as well as our spiritual growth over time. We should develop qualities and abilities that characterize God through spiritual maturity.

Through Christ, we are made new creations in God's likeness. By our faith in Him, we once again become partakers of His divine nature and more accurately reflect His image. Remember, God is spirit, and His physical image is unknown, but three virtues define his spiritual character—faith, hope, and love. As we journey through time pursuing God's purity and growing closer to Him, we'll develop a more robust character. Putting faith, hope, and love into action in our lives will help us become more like Jesus Christ, the part of God who came to earth to show us how to live. We must practice spiritual discipline by praying and reading our Bibles regularly to strengthen our ability to hear and trust Jesus, no matter what. Redemption from the sin that separates us from God is available only by God's grace through faith in Jesus Christ as our Savior.

First Adam and Second Adam

There's an apparent difference between the first Adam and the second Adam. After the first Adam sinned and caused humanity to be cursed, there was need for a second Adam to redeem the first Adam. Through the first Adam, the curse came to an understanding, and thus there was a need for the second Adam to deliver humanity from the evil of the first Adam's curse.

- The first Adam sinned, and humanity was cursed. The second Adam became the curse for the first Adam's deliverance and salvation.
- Adam, the first man, is of the earth. Jesus, the second man, is Lord from heaven.
- The first Adam sinned. Jesus, the second Adam, committed no sin.
- Through the first Adam, sin entered the world. Through Jesus, the second Adam, righteousness entered the world.
- The first Adam's sin separated us from God. The righteousness of Jesus, the second Adam, brought us back to God.

- Death came through the first Adam. The second Adam becomes the life-giver, the life and the resurrection.

The totality of the quality for humanity is written. The last Adam is a life-giving spirit, a quickening spirit to revive humanity and bring kindness and love towards understanding. Jesus was born as a human while still being totally divine. The concept of the humanity of Jesus coexisting with His deity is difficult for the finite mind of man to comprehend. Nevertheless, Jesus's nature—wholly man and wholly God—is a biblical fact. Some people, such as the Ebionites and Docetists, reject these biblical truths and declare that Jesus was a man but not God, but such viewpoints are unbiblical and false.

The humanity of Jesus is as essential to the Christian faith as his deity. New Testament teaching and the orthodox Christian position regarding the person of Christ is that Jesus is both God and man in the fullest sense of those words. In His person is a union of two distinct natures, human and divine, but His humanity and divinity did not combine to produce a unique third kind of life, nor did He have a dual personality. Instead, Jesus was a person with two natures. Jesus is truly human in every essential aspect and yet sinless, the most authentic human being who ever lived.

Only as a man could Jesus truly represent humanity to God. He understands our lives, because He lived as we do. Because Jesus understands firsthand the unsettling nature of daily life and the reasons behind our actions, we can go to Him to obtain mercy and grace to help in times of need. As a man, having experienced the pitfalls of humanity coupled with Satan's spiritual wickedness, Jesus provided for us a pattern for living as men and women. Jesus had to be born human for several reasons. He had to know what it felt like to be subjected to human authority and control, and He needed to experience the power, inspection, guidance, and instruction of a government that challenged humanity. He had to undergo the effects of the act of will to endure distress, pain, and death.

God inside a human body is subject to disability and handicap, but He remains God. But as a man, Jesus knew what emotions felt like and bore up those who suffered damage, injury, loss of income, and spiritual death with acts of love. This example in love is the pattern for living that Jesus ascribes to humanity—make amends for the guilt incurred by someone for something said or done, in or out of love, allowing forgiveness to demonstrate sorrow and repentance for the sin. Jesus, being both human and divine, is the ultimate representative of humanity who is susceptible to the sympathies and frailties of human nature. He can fulfill the law and implement grace, without grace ever being used up or destroyed, through His everlasting kingdom.

Jesus was born of a woman, under the law that solidified His human nature while also putting Him in a position to confirm the new and better covenant. People under the law were obligated to keep the law in all its aspects, and if they did not, the law condemned them. The problem was that no one was able to be justified by keeping the law, because no one could follow it entirely. The law of Moses can teach about God and man, but it can't be used as the means of sanctification, nor can anyone demand that others subject themselves to the provisions of the law.

There are 613 provisions to the law, all the do's and don'ts on moral and civil behavior as revealed in the first five books of the Old Testament. Humanity faced situations that could not be avoided, and clearly a redeemer was needed—*the* Redeemer, Jesus. He taught by example how to live, and He taught that forgiving past sins leads to a new life of love and holiness. We were kidnapped spiritually by Satan, the adversary of God and humanity, and held captive by the effects of our sins. The law covered sin but could not wholly exonerate us.

An older man lives in a house in the middle of the block, and at two thirty in the afternoon, he comes out to watch the high school girls pass by. He picks out certain girls and intimidates them with sinister smiles and stares. On occasion, he beckons for them to come toward him. One day the man suffers a heart attack in his front yard and dies. The children still pass his house as they walk to school, and although they know that the old man is dead, the sight of the house revives the man in their minds. As they begin walking pass the house, they talk not about the man, but about his house. The house is put on the market, but buyers are reluctant to buy because of the gossip concerning the house not the man.

The house is an inanimate object, not a living thing. It lacks cells that grow, metabolization, respond to no external stimuli, reproduces nothing, and no adaptation. The house cannot take responsibility for the man's actions or be deemed guilty by association with him. The house is associated with the man's behavior, but he's now dead and separate from the house. To forgive the older man for his bad behavior is good, but to harbor unforgiveness against him will make people grow physically ill and age faster than normal. The house is an object to displaced blame and the focus of forgiveness of the old man is lost in the displaced focus. Unforgiveness is a scheme and trickery of Satan which keep the righteous from God.

Jesus's redemption relieves us of the responsibility, obligation, and hardship of keeping the law and clears us from accusations, blame, judgment, and condemnation based on the law. The first Adam plunged us into sin through disobedience, and the law was established to facilitate order, the pathway back to God. God in His infinite knowledge gave us the right to choose; however, with choice comes the knowledge of good and evil, and emotions enters our decision-making processes.

How can we know what we do not know? The absence of spiritual knowledge lacks the essence and substance of religious experience. Satan knows that we do not understand the nature of spiritual knowledge, and our ignorance gives him the power to control our actions and emotions with what seems right to us but is actually ungodliness. Satan apprehends the inner nature of things, and he knows that breaking the law creates separation between God and the sinner, which results in death. He devises untruths and uses them to his advantage in our humanitarian performances related to our right to choose, so that tasks that seem to be right are conscious and moral schemes of death.

The sin unleashed on humanity in the garden could be covered but not eradicated. The sins of people under the law could be covered with the blood of sacrificed animals, but that blood did not pay the debt. Imagine the incalculable amount of blood that was needed to bring life back to dead souls which provided a temporary covering for sin. That same blood only foreshadowed the perfect and complete sacrifice. Without the shedding of blood, there is no forgiveness.

The first death came when God sacrificed animals and made clothes out of the skins for Adam and Eve. The deaths of the animals had to be horrific for Adam and Eve, for within their union the first human deaths occur on earth and probably graphic demonstrations.

After the sin was committed in the Garden of Eden, Adam

and Eve discovered they were naked. A metaphor for their spiritual death and a foreshadowing of things to come. Their covering was accomplished by the shedding of animal blood from the death of the animals and their skins were made for coverings, clothes to cover Adam and Eve to cover their nakedness.

Animal sacrifice was a symbolic ritual in which the blood represented life and was drained from the animal as a reminder to the worshipper of death. There were many symbolic ways the sacrifices were made to represent cleansing. As a scapegoat, one goat was slaughtered and another released into the wild, metaphorically carrying away the sin of Israel. The sprinkling of blood around the temple represented life cleansing the death of sin, since blood was a symbol of life.

The Israelites, the chosen people, were instructed to build a temple among them as God's dwelling place. Inside the temple was a particular part that almost no one could enter, the Holy of Holies, where God's presence dwelled. This section of the temple was curtained off and could be entered only once a year by the high priest. Before he entered the Holy of Holies, the high priest would tie a rope around his ankles, so that his body could be pulled out if God's glory struck him dead for being inadequately cleaned. The Holy of Holies is where the Ark of God, a gold-covered wooden chest with a lid cover containing two stone tablets, the Ten Commandments, rest. This chest is also known as the Ark of the Covenant.

Moses could not gaze fully on God's face and live, and anyone who touched the Ark of the Covenant instantly fell dead. Not only was humankind separated from God, but sinful man could not stand in the presence of God's holiness and live. God made a covering for the first couple to cover their nakedness, although they were still sinful. Blood was shed because of their sin, so God instituted sacrifice, which became a recurring theme.

God works through humanity. He ensures that we understand and appreciate Jesus Christ, who was revealed in the flesh and came to earth not just to reveal God to us, but also to reveal us to ourselves. The fullness of time had come for Him to be revealed to the world as both a true God and a true man. We're speaking about the Redeemer, Jesus Christ, the Son of the living God. To everyone who receives Him as Lord and believes in His name as our savior, He gives the right to become children of God. For those who are born not of flesh and blood or the will of man, but of God, He chooses to speak of them as adopted as well as being children by new birth. Because we are His children, God has sent the Spirit of his Son, the Holy Spirit, into our hearts, crying, "Abba! Father!" We're no longer slaves, but God's children and heirs. When we did not know God, we were enslaved to those who by nature are not gods, including Satan.

Jesus Christ redeemed us from sin, purchasing us by paying a steep ransom. The first Adam sold us into slavery to sin and death, and because everybody after him was imperfect, nobody could buy back what he had lost. Jesus's sacrifice is how God delivered us, saving humankind from sin and death. Jesus was the ransom for many.

- The ransom involves payment. The price was the blood of Jesus, with which Jesus bought people for God out of every tribe, tongue, people, and nation.
- The ransom brings about redemption. Jesus's sacrifice provided a release by ransom from sin.

- The ransom corresponds to the value of what is paid for. Jesus's sacrifice corresponds precisely to what Adam lost—perfect human life. Just as through the disobedience of Adam, many were made sinners, so also through the obedience of Jesus Christ, many will be made righteous.

Jesus's sacrifice is a corresponding ransom for all those who take the steps necessary to benefit from it. Christians hold fast to the gospel by nature as the children of violence, anger, and disobedience, but by grace, they become children of love partaking of the nature of the children of God, for He will have all His children resemble Him. All God's children shall have the inheritance of eldest sons. May their temper and conduct show our adoption and may the Holy Spirit witness with our spirits that we are children and heirs of God.

The second Adam, Jesus Christ, became the Passover Lamb— the propitiation and atoning sacrifice—for the Christian church, for without the sacrifice of Jesus Christ, we have no forgiveness, no hope, and no assurance on the pathway to God.

With no blemishes, Jesus alone had sufficient worth to die in place of every mortal in history. Everything before Him was preparatory to His perfect sacrifice. This is true under

- His deity,
- His acceptance of suffering to be made perfect
- His superiority to Moses
- His ability to provide an eternal Sabbath rest for God's people; God's call of Him as a priest in the order of Melchizedek
- His establishment of a perpetual priesthood

- His presence at God's right hand as an eternal priest, after offering a perfect sacrifice
- His superiority to the Aaronic priesthood of animal sacrifice
- His ability to carry the results of His sacrifice into heaven itself, not merely into the Holy of Holies
- His once-for-all-perfect sacrifice for sin; and
- His willingness to be the sacrifice, not merely for one but all.

Only Jesus's blood could roll back to the first sinner and forward to the last. Whatever temporary measure God used before Christ's birth to secure forgiveness and atonement, Jesus alone was slain, in God's mind, as the perfect sacrifice for sin. That's why death exalted Jesus from being a mortal Jew to being the universal Lord. When God tore the veil leading into the Holy of Holies in two, He ripped it from the top to the bottom when Jesus died, it meant that Jesus Christ's death opened for us an unobstructed pathway to God.

We must understand the wilderness temple of God. Moses's temple of God was a wilderness tabernacle, God's dwelling place that housed the Ark of the Covenant. The temple grounds were inside an enclosure divided into two sections, the first section is called of the outer court and its equipped with an alter and laver. The second section in the yard is called the inner court and it has a structure called the tabernacle which has two rooms. The first room inside the tabernacle is called the Holy place and the second room is called the Most Holy Place.

Within the outer court, the high priest would sprinkle the blood of a sacrificed bull or a goat upon the alter to make amends for his and the people's sins. The flesh of the dead animal was burned on the alter. Also, in the outer court was the laver filled with water used for cleansing. The outer court was where sin was symbolically burned and washed away before the priest went any further in the atonement rites.

After being cleansed, the priest went through a door into the first room, the Holy Place of the tabernacle. In this room were three objects: a table with the shewbread, a table with seven candlesticks, and an altar with incense.

The table for the shewbread was made of acacia wood—three feet long, eighteen inches broad, and two feet three inches high—and plated with pure gold. Shewbread was consecrated, unleavened bread made of the finest flour and prepared flat and thin. The shewbread was placed on the table in two rows of six each, representing the twelve tribes of Israel. The shewbread was replaced every Sabbath, and the old shewbread was eaten by the priests in the holy place. Another table held the twelve candlesticks, one for each tribe of Israel, and the altar held incense that filled the room with thick smoke.

Between the Holy Place and the sacred most holy chamber—the Holy of Holies was a thick, embroidered veil with cherubim motifs woven directly into the fabric separating the two chambers. Housed in the Holy of Holies chamber was the Ark of the Covenant—the Ark of God, the gold-covered wooden chest with a lid cover containing two stone tablets, the Ten Commandments. This sacred chest was made by the ancient Israelites according to the command and design of God.

Only one person could enter the chamber behind the veil, and he could do so only on the annual Day of Atonement. On that day, the high priest would bathe and put on the clean garments of the priesthood; his robe that had solid gold bells hanging from the hem. He entered the Most Holy Place with a censer of burning incense.

The thick smoke hid the mercy seat (the gold lid placed on the Ark of the Covenant) where God was, because anyone who saw God would die instantly.

The high priest was appointed by God to oversee the sacred responsibility of entering the Holy of Holies – the Most Holy Place on the annual Day of Atonement to atone for the sins of the people. The noise of the bells told the people he was making atonement for their sins. But if the bells did not sound, the priest was dead and had to be pulled out of the Most Holy chamber by the rope tied around his waist. Regular priests were allowed in the outer and inner courts, but the Holy of Holies – the Most Holy could be entered only by the priest appointed by God.

To conclude that God cannot look upon sin is to say that sin can defeat and defile God, that sin is more powerful than the righteous holiness of God. But God is not weak and powerless to sin, sinful natures, or Satan. When Satan comes into the presence of God, God is not threatened. God never looks upon wickedness with pleasure and approval. Be careful not to confuse God's refusal to approve sin with the idea that He does not use sinners or even Satan to accomplish His will.

Only the high priest was allowed to go before the Spirit of God behind the veil, once a year, carrying sacrificed animal blood to petition for himself and the people for their sins to be covered by the offering of the animal blood sacrifice. God honored Jesus's sacrifice with the victory of bodily resurrection through the cross as an object of pleasure for us and victory for Christ. Christ's death made a spectacle of all opposition to God. No further sacrifices were needed, so Christ's own perfect sacrifice eliminated the temple's relevance to cover sin.

We need neither trust our righteousness nor fear our sins. Christ's resurrection guaranteed our emancipation from sin while it obligated us to God's grace. Christ's sacrifice set us free from restraint, confinement, and servitude and proposed an end to a desire and behavior that causes trouble. There's nothing we can do to deserve grace, since Christ's resurrection verifies His sacrifice's sufficiency.

Jesus endured the cross by focusing His mind on one thing—the joy that awaited Him. He disregarded the shame of the cross, and now He sits in the place of honor beside God on God's throne. The cross was the most horrible event Jesus could have ever endured, but He did it without complaining about all who would later come to repentance. If there was ever anyone who didn't deserve the cross, it was Jesus. The cross was part of God's plan for Him to get possession of the salvation that we gloriously and freely possess today. Jesus plainly did not find enjoyment or delight in the experience, but He accepted His assignment from God.

God, the Veil, and God's People

Jesus's suffering began in the garden of Gethsemane, when God laid the sins of the world on Him. The human side of Jesus, during prayer with the Father, apprehended the inner nature of the cross and saw intuitively the difficult and precarious suffering to come. The intense stress caused hematidrosis, a condition in which blood seeps out of sweat glands, indicating the agony He faced as He went through with His Father's assignment. Jesus was arrested and flogged so mercilessly that His skin was stripped off His back, exposing muscle and bone. He was slapped, punched, crowned with thorns, beaten with reeds, and then covered with a red robe then led to Golgotha.

The Roman soldiers drove seven-inch nails into His wrists, probably hitting the nerves and causing blinding pain, then rammed other nails into His feet.

Hung on the cross, Jesus suffered dislocations of both shoulders, cramps and spasms, dehydration from severe blood loss, accumulated fluid in His lungs which can eventually cause lung collapse and heart failure. He chose to endure this pain for us by declaring that not His own will, but God's will be done. Hanging on the cross, Jesus was offered vinegar to drink, but he refused it saying, "It is finished." (John 19:30) Then He bowed His head and died, giving up the ghost. The agony was over, the terrible ordeal was finished, the race had been run, the work was completed, and the enemy Satan was defeated.

Physicians who have studied the description of Jesus's death say the pain would have been beyond excruciating. In fact, the pain was so great every breath taken was extremely painful, so painful the word *excruciating* literally describes the pain as, came out of the cross, an intense mental distress. Jesus defined it as the worst pain anyone could feel. Because of Jesus, the foundations of redemption were fully laid. Jesus dismissed His spirit from His flesh.

When Jesus died on the cross dismissing His Spirit, God tore the veil in the temple housing the Ark of the Covenant from the top to the bottom. Only God could have done that, because that veil was sixty feet tall and four inches thick. The direction of the tear symbolized God destroying the barrier between Himself and humanity, an act that only God had the authority to do. We have an open way through Christ to the throne of grace.

The tearing of the temple veil meant that God restored the priesthood of believers. Every follower of Christ can now approach

God directly, without the intervention of earthly priests. Christ, now the great High Priest, intercedes for us before God. When God looks upon us, He sees Jesus, our propitiation. All barriers have been destroyed through the sacrifice of Jesus on the cross. God dwells once more with and in His people through the Holy Spirit. Let us, with an eye of faith, behold Christ crucified and be affected with that great love with which He loved us. Never were the horrid nature and effects of sin so tremendously displayed as on that day when the beloved Son of the Father hung upon the cross, suffering for sin, the Just for the unjust, that He might bring us to God.

What must we do today to be saved?

- Believe that Jesus sacrificed His life for our sins. Believe that He was a real person and that all biblical accounts about him are accurate.
- Learn what the Bible really teaches, and then teach the word of God with accurate knowledge based on the scriptures.
- Repent and feel deep sorrow over previous wrong attitudes and conduct. Our repentance will be obvious to others as we stop practices that offend God and do works that befit repentance.
- Get baptized. Jesus said that those who become His disciples would gladly be baptized. They are taught the truth about Jesus and are the ones who accept His word.
- Obey Jesus instructions. People who observe all the things that Jesus commanded demonstrate through their lives that they are His followers and become doers of the word and not hearers only.

- Endure to the end. Jesus's disciples need endurance to be saved. One example of endurance was the apostle Paul, who maintained strict obedience to Jesus's teachings and loyalty to God from the day he became a Christian until he died.
- Engage in continuous prayer and worship.

What about the "Sinner's Prayer"? We are all sinners saved by grace. We are all imperfect and need the Holy Spirit to help keep us spiritually in God's will. In some religions, people say prayers such as the "Sinner's Prayer" and the "Salvation Prayer," etc. Typically, those praying acknowledge their sinfulness and express belief that Jesus died for their sins. They also ask Jesus to come into their hearts or their lives, but the Bible neither mentions nor recommends a formulaic sinner prayer.

Some people think that after expressing a sinner' prayer, a person is assured of eternal salvation, but no prayer guarantees salvation. As imperfect humans, we continue to make mistakes knowingly and unknowingly. That is why Jesus taught His followers to pray regularly for forgiveness of sins. Furthermore, some Christians in line for eternal salvation lose that prospect because they turn away from God with having too high an opinion of themselves.

Before the conversion of Saul to Apostle Paul by God Himself, Saul dealt plainly with those who urged the law of Moses together with the gospel of Christ. He endeavored to bring Christian believers under the bondage of the law by securing a writ from the government to persecute Christians. Christians did not fully understand the meaning of the law as given by Moses but that the ideology was a dispensation of darkness and bondage. They were tied to many burdensome rites and observances, by which they were taught and kept subject like children under tutors and governors. We learn the happier state of Christianity under the gospel dispensation. We see the wonders of divine love and mercy, particularly of God the Father in sending His Son into the world to redeem and save us by submitting so low to suffer so much for us and of the Holy Spirit who dwells in the hearts of believers for such gracious purposes.

The only thing God need from us is to believe in Jesus Christ. God created everything and owns everything, and He wants us to be good stewards over the possessions given us without selfishness. To please God is to exercise faith through belief in Jesus Christ and trust in Him, for in God's timing we shall reap what we sow.

Stewardship

We all were born into the world naked and then clothed with garments made from resources already provided for us. We ate the flesh of animals that were here before man and drank from the fountain of life, water rained down into the atmosphere from heaven. God made our mothers capable of sustaining life; whereby Adam called Eve the mother of all living.

God created Eve to be suitable for and worthy to Adam, not to be his possession, but to be his helper and companion on earth. In Hebrew, *helpmeet* means something more profound and powerful than just a helper, and when we understand what God was saying to Adam, we come to see Eve's role and the role of women on this earth in a different light. Eve was not designed to be exactly like Adam, but rather his mirror opposite, possessing opposite qualities, responsibilities, and attributes that he lacked. Just like Adam and Eve's sexual organs are mirror opposites, one being internal and the other external, the two people were designed to be opposite but fit together perfectly to create life. Eve was Adam's complete spiritual equal, endowed with an essential saving power that was opposite from his.

Although women do much to help and assist men in their stewardship, they have been given a stewardship that is uniquely theirs and every bit as important as that of men. Women are saviors to men by the fact that they give men life and nurture them toward the light of Christ. By conceiving, creating, and bearing mortal bodies, women make it possible for God's children to start on their mortal journeys with an opportunity to become perfected. Women provide a gateway into this world that allows for progress and exaltation.

In addition, women are willing to sacrifice their lives if necessary, to bring children into this world, thus demonstrating the true meaning of charity (love). From a child's very first breath, they are the recipients of charity and unconditional love. This is a powerful gift that a mother gives to her child, and it is her love that first points them toward Christ. Each woman, regardless of her ability to give birth or not, is a savior to mankind when she loves and nurtures a child to be closer to Christ.

Even Adam, whose physical body was not created by a daughter of Eve, was saved and delivered by a woman, for it was through Mary that Jesus Christ came to conquer the bonds of death and sin and atoned for Adam's transgression. Without a woman to bear the body of Christ, mankind would have fallen and lost forever, and Adam's work and purpose on earth would have been meaningless. Mary was the gateway that made Christ's work possible, and her nurturing was the catalyst for His success. Even though Eve didn't give physical life

135

to Adam, she literally saved him from spiritual death by opening the way for the Savior, the Redeemer to come into the world. Salvation, in the form of human and Christ, literally came to earth through a woman.

This perspective on Eve is different from what we normally hear about women's roles in the world. Understanding the real meaning of *helpmeet* will make a huge difference in how we understand the mission of women. If women could understand what a marvelous stewardship the Lord has given them, they would not waste so much time and energy being angry that they can't have a man's stewardship. True power comes when men and women understand that they have been blessed with different gifts, abilities, and stewardships, and that they could work together as equal partners to help each other become successful soul mates. Men and women need each other, and it is only when they are united—one body, one soul and one mind—that God's work moves forward. Men and women are nothing without each other and more with Christ. It is not good that men should be alone, so God made women to be their equals—they are strong companions who possess saving power. How different our world would be if men and women really understood that they need each other!

We're so busy doing work in somebody else's name that our lack of knowledge and understanding of God's purpose makes our prayers and the work we do self-serving. At times we interject our emotions into situations, creating turmoil to bring about the results we desire. Our emotions are at the center of what we want to achieve for ourselves, and then we give glory to God. If we don't achieve our desired outcomes, we change the situation and expect the results to change in our favor. If that happens, we then give glory to God. But if not, we just keep going around the same situation again and again.

For some of us, seeking God's knowledge—God's righteous way of doing something—seems too slow and boring. We're impatient, and we want results now. So we don't seek out God's purpose concerning the situation, but again, how can we know what we don't know if we don't seek God, but we seek Him with our own agenda in hand? We believe that it's necessary to base our decisions on logic and reasoning focused on worldly pursuits rather than on religion and spiritual affairs.

Shunning responsibility of spiritual pursuits and expressing gratitude toward others for providing unintelligent information related to God's character is sin. It's sinful for the person seeking the information and the person providing the information. Associating the Word of God with personal gain dulls the mind, whether we're the deliverer or the receiver. Such decisions result in someone acting defiantly or in an unintelligent and careless manner, which we then justify by blaming others. We hold to material items with much love rooted so deeply within our hearts that we mentally possess it warmly, sincerely, and earnestly. We embed people the same way into our hearts, and then we mentally destroy ourselves when the relationships are disturbed or broken.

Think about giving a toddler a toy, and the toddler finding joy in just possessing it. If you abruptly take the toy away, the child suddenly becomes quite disturbed. The toy has no value to the toddler except that he held it as property, and now it has been taken away and his life has been disrupted. The toddler lacks knowledge and understanding about the toy, which is why he becomes upset so easily. Not taking the toy away may have dire consequences, but the toddler cannot understand that. The situation can easily be resolved by replacing the toy with something else that the child wants and needs, such as a bottle of milk.

Are we like the first Adam in our disobedience? Adam was given stewardship over God's garden of Eden, and Eve was given stewardship over sustaining Adam with life—and they both failed. God has given us stewardship over our loved ones and material things, and we come to believe that we can hold on to them forever. God is working to achieve His purpose for humanity, though we have little knowledge of Him doing so. But as we experience life situations, our emotions are obliterated, as far as we're concerned, when someone die or we suffer significant material loss.

The last Adam, Jesus, was victorious over sin, flesh, and the devil. As a result, believers in Christ Jesus stand justified, redeemed, and spiritually wealthy liberated from sin and included in the adoption paradise of God – receiving immortality in the very presence of God himself. The paradise of God is where the faithful and anointed believers will be peaceful and joyous where they are rewarded to eat of the tree of life in the heavenly realm free from Satan and his emps.

The first Adam disobeyed God, but the last Adam was obedient unto death, even the death on the cross. If we believe and obey Jesus, the last Adam, praying through Him and according to God's will, everything will be added unto us. The choice is ours. Are you going to believe Jesus Christ? Jesus is faithful!

The first Adam gave life to all his descendants. The last Adam, Jesus Christ, communicates life and light to all people, and gives eternal life to those who receive Him and believe on His name, giving them power to become the sons of God.

Everyone needs to grow as Christians. We can all do so by simply applying the Bible principles of developmental growth through Jesus by faith, belief, and trust. We must not conform any longer to the pattern of this world but be transformed by the renewing of our minds. We must do our best to present ourselves to God as approved workmen, needing not to be ashamed and correctly handling the word of truth. Scriptures are God's breath, useful for teaching, rebuking, correcting, and training in righteousness, so that the men and women of God may be thoroughly equipped for every good work. As we walk step by step with the Spirit of God, applying God's Word to our lives, we will grow spiritually.

Spiritual maturity should be a priority. Anyone who lives on milk, like an infant, is not acquainted with the teaching about righteousness. Solid food is for the mature, who by constant use have trained themselves to distinguish good from evil. As believers, we are not to be milk fed; instead, we are called to chew on the meat of God's Word. We must discover God's truth through in-depth Bible study, feeding ourselves spiritually and then applying that sustenance to our lives as we walk with the Holy Spirit.

We must also understand that growth in spiritual maturity comes by grace, and God alone is our resource. Through God's divine power, He has given us everything we need for life and godliness, within the knowledge of Him who called us into His own glory and goodness. God has given us His great and precious promises, so that through them, we may participate in the divine nature and escape worldly corruption caused by evil desires.

Let us make every effort to add goodness to our faith; and to goodness, knowledge; and to knowledge, self-control; and to self-control, perseverance; and to perseverance, godliness; and to godliness, brotherly kindness; and to brotherly kindness, love. For if we possess these qualities in increasing measures, they will keep us from being ineffective and unproductive in our knowledge of our Lord Jesus Christ. Without these attributes, we are nearsighted and blind, having forgotten that we have been cleansed from our past sins.

When we became children of God, we were given all we needed in Christ to become spiritually maturing believers. However, we are liable and will be called to give an account of our godly contributions to humanity as the primary reason for being accepted into God's paradise after our transition from flesh into our spiritual bodies. Our choice—to either remain worldly or mature spiritually—must be made while we are living inside the flesh and there's still time to come into our eternal home. Let's choose to apply God's principles for our lives today to enjoy heaven on earth. The wonderful thing about being in submission to God's maturing process is that we will be changed!

God does the changing through His Word. We begin to talk like Jesus, walk like Jesus, do the things Jesus did the way He did them, forgive like Jesus, embrace like Jesus, and love like our Father, God. God's Word will transform us by the renewing of our minds, proving to us what is good, acceptable, and perfect. At the same time, we must humbly surrender our will to His Holy Spirit, adhering to the instructions within our hearts, not our heads. Our transition from flesh to spiritual will be made sure with comfort and no regrets. Giving an account of our stewardship, having learned of Jesus, our works are profitable to the kingdom of God according to His purpose.

Growing in spiritual maturity includes serving others in love. Inharmoniousness places barriers between civilizations and inserts schisms among the people. Many Jews greatly disliked Samaritans and Gentiles, whom they thought were beneath them. Struggles involving religion were constructed and dictated by learned scholars, and the law was interpreted by people who applied the law based on their own scholastic aptitudes. The timing of the four hundred years of God's silence was right, because the mark had truly been missed. God's proclamation of the gospel of the kingdom of God, as foretold by the Old Testament prophets, was shifting. Satan had a foothold, but he would be defeated by the One, the offspring of a woman. As God said in the beginning, the Messiah would be from within the lineage of David.

Satan's spirit is reigning on earth, and he goes after whomever he can devour. His ambition is to destroy everything God has made. He is powerless, but he's crafty enough to cause calamity wherever, whenever, and with whomever when the opportunity arises. He lies and causes conflict, hostility, disagreement, disharmony, and dissension. People cannot see him to fight him because they don't know when he's present and attacking them. He attacks the mind with his craftiness, orchestrating man's demise.

There was a little girl whose Christianity began maturing at an early age. Her family members were raised in the church, where they learned about God. Throughout her young life, she enjoyed Christian living. In her early teens, she experienced the wiles of the world, though she kept returning to God. In her clubbing days, this young woman and her cousin, who had also grown up in the church, were running buddies. But when the young woman met her future husband—a wonderful, God-fearing man—her desire for clubbing lessened as she began walking in the light of Jesus. Soon club time turned into husband-and-wife time, and they began building a relationship with God through Jesus. Building that relationship took time, but the young woman and her cousin continued to talk and interact frequently.

The woman's husband eventually retired from his city street department job, but within two years he got cancer and began losing weight. As his illness worsened, the woman had to relinquish some of her job responsibilities to take care of him. Her husband had a host of relatives and friends, but they began to drift away as he got sicker, and some stopped coming around altogether. The husband's cancer began taking a grave toll on him, but the woman singlehandedly met the challenge of keeping him lively, fed, clean, and comfortable.

The United States government stepped in to provide hospital care. The woman had to travel to another state for her husband to receive this care. The woman frequently packed up her husband into their SUV and drove him to the doctor. The medical staff determined that her husband had inoperable brain cancer, and he was losing his memory and bodily functions. There was nothing they could do to stop the cancer's growth or revive the dead cells in his brain. The woman's siblings, friends, and coworkers stepped up to help, enabling her to rest and continue working. Her husband's family members did nothing to help, showing up at the end only to watch him die. The woman's cousin also reappeared. She too was there when the husband died.

Although the woman and her cousin had remained close, the cousin was not open and true in her relationship with God, allowing Satan to rise. The cousin chose clever and underhanded means of achieving her goals, risking the love of her family and friends. She would become discombobulated concerning relationships and then shut down her associations, closing out people and then blaming them for failing to understand her. She would become antisocial and wouldn't answer her phone or return calls. She would shut people out until she was satisfied that she had hurt them enough, then she'd allow them access to her again. After she'd decide to open up, she'd blame the other people for her issues and meltdown.

Now on his deathbed, the lady's husband moved his lips, but no sounds emerged. He stared into space through glassy eyes, as if his attention were focused on something in the room, but there was nothing there. The mood in the room was filled with sadness and regret as the woman's husband slipped out of consciousness and into eternity.

The next day, a group assembled at the woman's house. The cousin came in, sipping wine from a glass. The woman playfully said to her, "You brought only one glass of wine?"

The cousin replied with intentional rudeness, "This was my last bottle of wine," and then she immediately shut down. After a few moments, she left.

The woman phoned her cousin later that day to discuss her husband's funeral arrangements, but the cousin didn't answer, so she left a message. The woman tried calling her cousin several times that day, but she never got an answer. She suspected her cousin knew she was calling because of the caller ID but had no intentions of answering the phone.

The woman began to wonder what she had done to cause her cousin to treat her like this. She sat down in despair reflecting on the journey that had led to her husband's death and began to cry. Adding into her grieving equation, what had she done to unsettle her cousin at such a critical time in her life? Everything was crashing in just as she had lost her husband. Was it because she teased about the wine?

The woman became agitated. Her husband was now dead and none of his family had helped her with his care. Now she was left alone with hurtful memories. She had taken unpaid time away from her job to care for her husband. The medical bills had mounted up and they were still coming in. Now there's a household of one with years of fond memories and tears, and a funeral to pay.

Tired, the woman decided not to put up with her cousin's ridiculous ways any longer. The woman had suffered repeatedly from her cousin's bad attitude, and this was not a time for another issue. Her cousin's foolishness indicated a lack of common sense and sound judgment. The woman decided that the next time she saw her cousin, she was going to . . . Her words had gotten vulgar and sharp as her anger mounted, and now she was crying from hurt and disgust.

After an hour or so had passed, and the woman's venting calmed her down. In the quiet, she heard the Spirit of God. She received the truth about whose she was and who her Father is. She was reminded about why Jesus had suffered, died, and risen and is seated at the right hand of the Father in heaven. She realized that Satan was trying to take advantage of her during this vulnerable time by telling her that her husband was dead and now she was alone—but the truth is that she hadn't lost him. The Spirit of God reminded her, she had been a good steward of God's possession. The nurturing and caring for her husband while he had gone through that long bout of sickness as his wife made for a good steward. Be mindful death was secured for all humanity in the garden of Eden by Adam, but Jesus Christ has conquered death by His resurrection. He who was dead is now alive because of what was accomplished on the cross. Jesus death, burial, and resurrection solidified our pathway back to God through our godly characteristic lifestyle to an eternal heaven. God required her husband's soul thus he transitioned.

The woman remembered that God said to love her neighbor as herself, and she had given everything possible to fulfill her husband's needs. Likewise, her family and friends were responsible for making her comfortable. As she remembered her husband's last words of endearment to her, she smiled. Those words had been soothing and peaceful, then he passed on.

Satan had attempted to make a moment of endearment morally objectionable. He will use any method and take any opportunity to turn God's people away from righteousness in Christ Jesus. Satan got the woman's cousin to focus exclusively on herself without any regard for others. We could excuse her by saying that she lacked knowledge, education, and awareness, but she had been raised in a family with strong Christian values that she could have used to defeat Satan. Unfortunately, she had allowed Satan to furnish her with other values as well, including stupidity.

God had a reason for creating us, and as we know, we must take on His character to journey through life righteous. Our journey is filled with obstacles to keep us from God, but Jesus has defeated Satan therefore, we must hold true to Jesus to show us the way to God. We must rely on the Holy Spirit to help us get there.

The word *stupid* can be defined as having a lowliness of mind given to unintelligent decisions or acting in an unintelligent and careless manner. This definition fit the cousin, because she had the knowledge but lacked the intelligence to be loving. The Holy Spirit spoke to her heart, but her heart had hardened, so she relied on worldly knowledge sanctioned by Satan.

A person can cause trouble and bother people with the intent to serve without dignity and honor. Having a lowness in mind or the absence of knowledge doesn't necessarily reflect a harmful intent. In Jesus's righteousness and the help and comfort of the Holy Spirit, we have an example of the truth and love of our Father God. Compassion for one another stems from love, and righteousness yields forgiveness and prompts us to teach God's character in our words and deeds.

On the other hand, being mean is a typical action for serving with an attitude of stupidity. Mean actions are intended to cause a person pain, suffering, and discomfort. To treat people meanly indicates an inferior quality and status, lacking in mental discrimination, dignity, and honor. To be mean and stupid is to occupy a middle position between two extremes—God and Satan—and to stand between resources available for disposal of unclean things and material resources affording a secure life or death. There's no middle ground in life, only the extremes. God requires that we choose one extreme, and He tells us to choose life, as a good Father would. God said He would spit from His mouth anyone not fully committed to Him.

Satan used the cousin in a familiar role, at a moment when the woman was vulnerable. The cousin didn't realize that she was being used to fill the woman's heart with hatred and anguish. For about an hour, the woman didn't want to hear a word of truth. She fought the truth with her emotions—regarding not only her cousin, but also her husband's family members. She held them all accountable for not helping her as she worked hard to care for her husband.

After the woman had vented for an hour, the Spirit of God spoke the truth directly into her heart and calmed her down. What He said is not important, but we can stand assured that He said something. But through her prayer, she forgave not only her cousin but everybody who might have had any responsibility for helping care for her husband. She asked God to forgive her for hurting or blaming anyone verbally, implied, or in thought, whether she had realized it or not.

The next day the woman received an abundant blessing that could have come only from God. Satan meant this episode for bad, but God turned it into good, and He got all the glory from her in praises and testimonies. The young woman could not see the blessing God had in store for her, but if she had continued in her anguish and hatred, she would have missed the blessings. By faith she continues to journey through life believing God, trusting in Him.

As for the cousin, God still showers her with His grace and mercies, because He still loves her. She doesn't know how much time she's got to acquire God's character traits and to walk in truth, only God know her date of transition.

God's covenant agents, Adam and Eve, were tempted by Satan. They accepted the lie and fell out of fellowship with God. All are affected by sin, but God didn't break His covenant with creation. Through Jesus came a better covenant and with the help of the Holy Spirit to guide us to God, who will never leave us nor forsake us. Time is running out.

CHAPTER 7

Soft-Spoken Whisper

God spoke
the heavens and the earth into existence.
He spoke to His people,
But the people stopped listening.
Four hundred years of silence?
The written Word spoke!
God is still speaking.
Period.

ONCE UPON A TIME, A man went to see his ten-year-old son at his ex-wife's home, which had been purchased during their seven-year marriage. The boy had phoned his dad to share the news about a school program in which he was excelling. He was excited to tell his dad about his achievement and show him the awards. The boy had done most of the talking, but he had also been overwhelmed with joy at talking to his dad, whom he missed very much.

The man arrived at the ranch-style house and parked at the front curb, careful not to block the driveway or park on the grass. He rang the doorbell, and his son opened the door and leaped into his arms. After the hugs, then the boy invited his dad inside, the man hesitantly asked, "Is your mother home?"

"No," said the boy. "Come on in!"

Reluctantly, the man said, "I don't think I ought to come in, son. Why don't you come out, and we can talk out here?"

The boy replied comfortably, "Mommy said for me to stay in the house, so come on in!"

Instead, the man stood on the porch and asked about his son's friends, school, sports, and the like. They were having a good time until the boy began talking about the special programs. He then went into the house and got the awards to show his dad. Their discussion turned toward the boy learning typing skills and becoming computer literate. Suddenly, like a light switch had flipped on in the boy's mind, he said enthusiastically, "Daddy, come inside. I'll show you my computer."

The man felt a deep, poignant distress caused by his uncertainty about his ex-wife's reaction if she arrived home and found him inside. His excitement went into a downward spiral. He suddenly felt quite melancholy. He tried to explain to his son why it wasn't a good idea for him to be in the house when the boy's mother arrived. He was afraid that her bitterness toward him would cause her to be upset with both him and their son.

As a police officer, the man was skillful at defusing hostile situations. His work ethic and professionalism were excellent, he had caught his ex-wife in an adulterous relationship. His professional skills as a well-trained investigator, coupled with his calm demeanor, meant that he was certain of his investigative conclusions. Fourteen years as a police officer had given him skills that were useful socially as well as on the job. His wife became furious and turned the blamed on him for her outside relationship. She was outdone by him catching her while she had thought the extra-marital relationship was well hidden. He waited until all the facts were irrefutable before he confronted her. That's where her bitterness came from, and she refused him reasonable visitation of the children as revenge.

The man knew that if his ex-wife arrived while he was in the house, she'd be difficult to deal with. The son didn't understand why his father kept refusing. The boy began begging, pleading, squirming and tugging on his father's arm, trying to pull him into the house. "Come on, Daddy. She won't know. She's not here. You can be gone before she gets back!"

The man could see why it meant so much to his son for him to go inside the house. They had been really close. The man had been in and out of his son's life for nearly two years, seeing him only a few times. The boy wanted to impress upon his father with all his school achievements. The man's mind began working to justify going inside and checking out what his son wanted to show him. But in his heart, the Spirit kept saying no.

The boy's persistent pleading was crushing the man's heart. The man's resistance was running low. His son's eyes filled with tears, and his voice sounded defeated as he succumbed to brokenness. This was hard for the man. He couldn't bear to see his son defeated right before his eyes. They had been so close. The father was his son's strength. The son liked to mimic his father, but now the man was feeling his son's pain—and it weighed in heavily. The man's mind was trying to persuade him to do a quick in and out, but the Spirit of God spoke within his heart and told him again, "Don't go in there!"

The voice inside the man's head said, *"go in the house, quickly, check out the computer, and get out before she gets home."* Finally, he surrendered and told his son to quickly show him the computer, and immediately the boy's mood flipped once again from miserable to joyful. They went into the dining room, and there in the corner was the boy's computer. The son showcased feature after feature while his father stood watched in awe.

They hadn't been there more than five minutes when the man's ex-wife walked into the house. Her shocked reaction was reminiscent of her displeasure at being caught with her boyfriend. She angrily criticized them both—the man for being in the house, and the boy for allowing him inside—but she was most brutal, mentally and emotionally, on their son. The man tried to shift the blame on himself, but she knew that inflicting pain on their son would devastate his father. She attacked the boy ruthlessly. Her harsh language was degrading, and as the man moved toward the door, he told himself, *"If only I had not come in ... I should have listened to the Spirit of God."*

There are many spirits, but there is only one Spirit of God who will guide us into all truth. The spirit of Satan comes to steal, kill, and destroy through diverse schemes. This man should have leaned on the strength of the Word of God and relied on the Holy Spirit to guide him. God told Malachi, "And he shall turn the hearts of the fathers to the children, and the heart of children to their fathers, lest I come and smite the earth with a curse." (Malachi 4:6)

But to those who reverence God's name; the Son of Righteousness, Jesus, will arise with healing wings. Those who reverence His name shall go forth and grow as calves in the stalls. We can't know God's timing—when or how He will work out a situation—so we must simply trust that He will.

Calves in their stalls are protected by the Lord. Because Jesus is the shepherd, we shall not want. We shall trust only in Him and walk by faith, not by sight. The Lord will make a way, and we must absolutely trust Him in our filth and guilt. Reverencing Jesus as Lord, our hearts will be reunited with our children by the Son of Righteousness's healing wings hovering above us and shielding us from deadly attacks. Happy are the calves in their stalls, because they're protected from predators. Similarly, we're furnished food and water regularly with sustained victory free from sin.

One essential key to experiencing freedom from sin is learning to live in the power of God's Holy Spirit. The Spirit plays a vitally important role in our lives, and we cannot afford to ignore Him or take Him for granted. The Holy Spirit enables us to "mortify the deeds of the body," (Roman 8:13) and He infuses us with the power to make decisions based on the righteousness of God. We're instructed to keep Satan under our feet and not to fight against him; he's a ruler and will rise to the challenge. We should not negotiate with him, because his interest is not with us; his actions and methods are planned and used to achieve particular goals leading to our death. He will willfully grant us the things we desire to His satisfaction.

However, not everything that we desire is free from moral corruption, sinister connections, errors, blemishes, or external hindrances toward kingdom living. The ramifications of our desires have mysterious components that affect other people's perceptions, senses, and mental capabilities in a way that does not accurately reflect our individual strengths. Our desires, being out of sight, are not readily apparent to others. That's the danger of them being unseen, unknown, not easily found out or recognized, unclean or impure, morally unclean or corrupt, disagreeable, distasteful, or objectionable. If we have no foreknowledge, we could fall into one or more of the corrupt faults. If we're made to believe that one or more of these ill conditions does not exist or affect our decisions, we may proceed in our endeavors. The result may be a spiritual or physical death.

The Son of Righteousness has a voice through the Holy Spirit, who speaks in a soft-spoken whisper. He speaks directly into our hearts. He was present when the boy and his father began their conversation at the front door. He was speaking to the father the entire time that Satan was wrestling with his mind. Satan provided the man with a scheme to satisfy the man and his son, but one that was against righteousness.

Satan made his scheme appear more attractive by acknowledging how good God is and suggesting that God would not allow the man to get caught inside the house. Surely God would do something extraordinary to allow the man to check out his son's computer and get out of the house before his ex-wife got home. However, choosing to do so was not of God! Satan's message was disguised as the man's faith that God would not let him get caught.

Did the man expect that God would do something unrighteous and look the other way? For righteousness to be unrighteous, there must be middle ground. God said that we're either for Him or against Him, for there is no middle ground. We cannot be lukewarm—we're either hot or cold. The middle ground is the area of unseen danger, the unknown that's not easily found out or recognized. If we're made to believe that other conditions do not exist, we'll proceed in our endeavors.

Expecting God to look the other way to allow the man to satisfy his son's emotions and unhappiness is to condemn the mother with the separation of the family and the marriage. Neither the father nor his son was associated with the wife's decision to engage in an adulterous relationship, but the results created sin against God's covenant of marriage. That sin has its own set of results, and the actions and decisions to be made were in the hands of God. Those sins needed mending—not more discord.

Satan, the voice of discord, made David the Psalmist, think that God would afford him protection and make a way to engage Bathsheba in an act of adultery. Only Satan would have allowed the father to violate God's righteousness, tempt God, and violate his ex-wife's principles. And only Satan would have allowed the son and his mother to become separated from God.

Satan's strength is to prey on our weaknesses, our limited knowledge of God. He uses our lack of knowledge to fabricate road maps to our desired outcomes and then convince us that it will be so. He plots out schemes and then convinces us that we are doing the right things. God, with His infinite knowledge, allowed Jesus to have a human body so that He could know human emotions. Discharging His spirit from that body at the cross, solidified the Holy Spirit coming into the earth realm, who now guide us in all truths toward righteousness according to the knowledge of God. We cannot be deceived following our hearts, because God has infinite knowledge of yesterday, today, and tomorrow of everybody in His heart.

God is

- omniscient, having infinite awareness, understanding, and insight
- omnipotent, having unlimited power and authority
- omnipresent, being present in all places at the same time

Prayer

We should pray. Praying develops the person praying their own language and begins the process of communicating with God. Jesus taught us that when we pray, we should acknowledge who we are praying to, our Father, who is in heaven. Then pray acknowledging God's name holy "hallowed be thy name" dedicating Him to His sacred purpose to His permanent office. Praying that God's kingdom is coming lets Him know that you know His kingdom *is* coming and that His will shall be done, as it is in heaven, so on earth. We ought to ask God to give us our daily bread and forgive our sins, as we also forgive everyone who has sinned against us breaks the yoke of bondage upon us. Asking God to lead us not into temptation, but to deliver us from evil, is telling God that we cannot complete our Christian journey alone. We need His helper, the Holy Spirit. We must learn to pray God's will for our lives and learn about Him, and then we'll know how to pray and what to pray for.

How do we know what we don't know? The Holy Spirit is

the spring of all desires toward God, which are often more than words can utter. Being feebleminded, we would be overpowered by ourselves, but the Holy Spirit helps us in our weakness. We do not know what we ought to pray for, but the Spirit intercedes for us with groans that words cannot express. The Holy Spirit searches the hearts of the renewed mind, (the born-again Christian) and the will of his or her spirit. The will of God, God's right way of doing something, is inserted into the heart and the person become an advocate for God's cause between God and humanity. The Holy Spirit having a view of God's purpose speaks in a soft-spoken whisper into the heart thus the enemy cannot become effectual.

The Holy Spirit cultivates the godly character in us, changing us to be the people whom God intends us to be. It's also the Spirit who firmly establishes us with the inner strength to endure hard times.

Many people experience hard times that are devastating for them, and others might not be aware of it. Not knowing other people circumstances is why we must be sensitive toward one another. In caring for others, we must demonstrate to God that we are concerned about the same issues that He is. Many troubled and destitute people in the world are desperately crying out for affection based on admiration, acts of kindness, generosity, and other common interests.

When people are hungry, we don't pray for God to supply them with food—we feed them. Similarly, when people ask for spiritual food, we don't pray for God to deliver His spiritual food to them—we teach them the Word of God and pray with them. Some people confess that they're thirsty, but they're not in need of something to drink. So we don't pray asking God to supply them with a thirst-quenching beverage—we teach the cup of the suffering, humiliation, and the degradation from which Jesus drank. Jesus was immersed into this cup on an unimaginable scale through betrayal, trial, scourging and execution. We are to symbolically commune with Jesus as did His apostles realistically at the Last Supper before His crucifixion. We are reminded by Jesus to recall this final meal, bread and wine, to our remembrance which present faith is the work of the Holy Spirit. Holy Communion is what we should teach by which believers can have real heart felt relationships with Jesus Christ in His death.

We must constantly examine ourselves to determine our worthiness to commune with Jesus regarding His cup. We must examine our worthiness to take Communion, the unleavened bread representing Jesus's broken body and a liquid from the vine representing His shed blood. As we ingest the unleavened bread and the liquid of the vine, we are judging ourselves worthy for our salvation—that we're chastened of our Lord, that we're not ill judged, and that we're not to be condemned with the world.

The apostles describe this sacred ordinance by the knowledge revealed from Christ. The visible signs demonstrate what is eaten is an expression provided against any believer being deprived of the cup. These acts of the ordinance signifies the outward signs of Christ's body broken and shed blood, together supply all the benefits that flow from His sacrifice and death which are paramount to us hearing the soft-spoken whisper of the Holy Spirit. These actions we take are in remembrance of Christ and His suffering, sacrifice, and atonement. Those who partake of it are to take Him as their Lord and life, yielding themselves up to Him, and live dependent upon His essential nature as the Son of God.

Holy Communion is taken in remembrance of Christ to keep fresh in our minds His dying for us. Remember as well, Christ pleas to the Father for us in virtue of His death and He's with God at His right hand. When God looks upon us, He see the nature of Jesus. We're also to remember what Jesus attitude was in overcoming trials and tribulation. The tests will come into our lives, but the word of God reminds us that Christ has overcome the world. Plus, we have been raised with Christ to a new life wherefor the Father has equipped us with His word and placed His Spirit inside of us that we may have peace. Take courage, we celebrate God's grace in our redemption. We declare His death to be our life, the spring of all our comfort and hope. We're to glory in the declaration showing forth His death and plead it as our accepted sacrifice and ransom. The Lord's Supper is not an ordinance to be observed merely for a time, but to be continued as often as we hold it dear within our hearts.

The apostle explains the danger of receiving Holy Communion with an unsuitable frame of mind. We're not to engage into the communion while our minds suggest we keep up with the covenant averting sin and death professing to renew and confirm the covenant to God. The renewed mindset incurs great guilt and renders us liable to spiritual judgment. The partakers of the holy communion must have a firm wholehearted religious conviction for the existence of God as fact and should not be discouraged from attending at the holy ordinance. The Holy Spirit never intends to deter serious Christians from their duty to become one with the Lord, though Satan has often made communion ritually impure. He causes us to remove the mental manifestation of our physical might causing us to become devoid of resources and we gradually sink to the bottom. Christians are warned to beware of the temporal judgments with which God chastised His offending servants and many times punishes those whom He loves. It is better to bear trouble in this world than to be miserable forever.

By thoroughly searching ourselves to condemn our sins and set right what we find wrong, we stop divine judgments. Let us all look to ourselves, that we do not come to God's worship to provoke Him and bring down vengeance on ourselves.

First, we need a leading heart and a willing mind to accept equally, according to what a man has rather than what he doesn't have. Our abundance may supply another person's need, and their abundance may supply our want, so that there may be equality and so the person who has gathered a lot has no more than he needs, and the person who has gathered a little has no lack. God has put this earnest care into our hearts of His own accord, for charity through all the churches.

Many people lack a warm, safe place to lay their heads for the night and adequate clothing to protect them from the bone-chilling elements of winter. When people are sick, they need someone to care for them, and when they're in prison, they yearn to know that someone cares enough to visit them. There are so many reasons poverty exists in this world, and there are no easy answers to why so many of the world's people have so little of the necessary resources. Whether or not we understand the complex issues involved, we realize that God's paternal heart goes out to the advantaged as well as the disadvantaged. When we care for the hurting or the disadvantaged, we are in fact serving as unto God, and He will reward our kindness by supplying our needs through someone's acts toward us. It is not about money all the time; there are some things that money cannot buy.

God endows us with the ability to accomplish whatever task He asks of us. Whatever God asks, however formidable the task may appear, He promises to provide us with the resources we will need to complete the work. God's will is that we live in an eternal heaven, so while on earth, we learn to tap into His power source of strength to accomplish His tasks, no matter what the outcome of our natural lives may be. The Holy Spirit guides us into all truths until we are called to glory in God's timing. God's greatest attribute is that He will never set us up for failure.

In the story about the father and his son, before the father chose to go into the house to appease his son, he should have prayed and asked God for guidance to lead him into the truth to sustain him concerning this situation. Instead, he left himself open for Satan to plant sympathy in his mind. Then he couldn't hear the whisper in God's soft-spoken voice in his heart. Satan convinced the man that God would provide a window of opportunity and allow him to appease his son. In rendering gratitude to both, he, and his son, the father made his decision based on a lie, contrary to the character of God. We may not fully understand why things happen, and we may not always discern the full extent of God's promises. But if our faith is in God, the theology will fall into line, and we will learn that Jesus's promises will always come to pass according to His perfect plan and in His perfect timing. How much we know or do not know is immaterial. What counts in the end is that we believe God, trust, and obey.

Belief and Trust

Once upon a time, there were seven men, one man had sight and six men were blind who had never seen an elephant. The six blind men were led to an elephant and staged at different places around it. They touched the part of the elephant where they were staged and were asked what type of animal was it? After they had all felt the elephant, they gave different descriptions of what type of animal they thought it was depending on what part they had felt. If the men had had a meeting, they would have been able to piece the animal together correctly. The only one who knew that it was an elephant was the man with sight. The necessity of revelation of something we are not able to perceive correctly or adequately is true of God. Was Jesus, a mythological being who is partly divine and partly human, with an inferior deity, also God?

Jesus died, was buried, rose into a different life, and forty days later ascended to heaven. He was taken out of our dimension in a cloud. Jesus spoke and taught like He possessed original knowledge and not delegated authority in matters of theology and moral law. He talked about leaving the earthly realm to be with the Father in the heavenly realm, and He explained that the Holy Spirit would come into the earthly realm and represent the Father and Him in an intimate and personal way. Previously Jesus had been with us as a human, but now the Holy Spirit has come to dwell in us and lead us into all truth. Jesus could be with only so many people and traveled on foot, but the Holy Spirit can be with everyone at the same time.

Most people believed and honored Jesus, some believed the irrefutable proof, some did not believe, and others refused to acknowledge Him. The Old Testament stories were handed down from generation to generation, and they carried assurance that God was real, powerful, and alive. It's amazing how God used history to work out His progressive purposes. Though we are living in the days of God's supposed silence, with no inspired writers for more than two thousand years, we must look back to those four hundred silent years to realize God had already said all that needed to be said. It's time to change our characters to become like Him.

God's purpose has not ended, for sure. Hopelessness is still rampant. God is moving to fulfill the prophetic Word concerning His Son establishing His (God's) kingdom. How long from now? How close is He? Who knows? But what God has done for us in the past, He will do again as we approach the end times. The soft-spoken whisper will continually say, "I change not." God never stopped speaking; people stop listening.

In God's amazing providence, He stands revealed not in platitudes and universal abstract, but in a breathtaking narrative recorded for us in the Bible. The Bible is not written to solve every problem that arises, but it is a set of values that are good and can be assembled and incorporated, fulfilling a mandate set by God for every purpose. The biblical concepts and themes of the Old Testament are the basis of New Testament teaching and support for New Testament truths. Each of us has a personal testimony where God has stepped into our lives and done something supernatural.

The intertestamental period (the struggling times) was not a period of silence, but a time to reflect on who God is and His representation for humankind. His worshippers who reverence Him have experienced His kind and tender care, and He has always done well for them. God never stopped speaking in that soft-spoken voice, however the people found other measures to hold accountable for their success or the demise. They measured life by what happened yesterday for today's strategy for tomorrow. But without God's voice, life equates to old age and then death. Yesterday and today is not surety for tomorrow; yesterday has passed, today is present, and tomorrow is a mystery of uncertainty. The methodology of known to plan for tomorrow's harvest of the unknown, toward sustaining life is factual only to know the body becomes weaker until it cannot physically survive. A dark rain cloud coming in your direction does not mean you're going to get rained on, just take your umbrella with you.

The mind realizes birth, time, and death. How to plan for a harvest to sustain life is taught to the offspring to ensure the survival of future generations. Since there are no inspired writers to record the voice of God today, some people have decided God has stopped speaking. There are those who believe they have obtained humanity's lessons and do rely on those proven or failed experiences. But God has never stopped speaking nor teaching and if people would embrace God seeking His will for their lives, God's way, people would become spiritual profitable. People just stopped listening! Over time, the Word of God became distorted, and eventually people's follies were incorporated in their lives as a way of life, making the power of belief and trust a representation of something formed in the mind having no validity.

The Spirit of God spoke to the apostle Paul, who wrote to the Corinthian church that we are all one bread and one body, and that we're all partakers of that bread. In the Spirit, we all must partake of that one bread, nourishing ourselves with the fruit in that one Spirit. So let us eat of that bread, remembering that Jesus is the living bread that came down from heaven, and if anybody eats of that bread, they shall spiritually live forever with the Father. The bread Jesus gave to us is His flesh, and He gave it for the lives in this world. Here we see the significance of the self-examination of our worthiness for Holy communion. Therefore, every man and woman should examine themselves to be worthy of the bread because if it is eaten unworthily, they who eat, eat damnation to themselves, not discerning the Lord's body. Also, we cannot forbear the cup and the drink of that cup.

We need to ask ourselves if we're able to drink of that cup. Do we know what we're answering to? Are we able to drink of the cup Jesus drank of and be baptized with His baptism? Usually we answer out of ambition and say we are able!

If we don't know what we're asking for, then how do we know what we don't know? Are we answering yes out of the conviction of our faith? However, with that answer comes the responsibility of the God-like character in which Jesus walked, now by our faithfulness to things hoped for and the evidence of things not seen – the Holy Spirit teaches and leads us into all truths. Our responsibility to hear God within our heart becomes our mandate to fight Satan using trust and the power of God through the Holy Spirit as our strength. We are establishing the power of our faith through trust and belief.

In His deity, Jesus has been given all power in heaven and in earth by Father God. He's instructing us to move away from places and people to take certain courses and follow certain procedures to teach all nations baptizing them in the name of the Father, Son, and Holy Ghost. This incorporates the whole design of the Christ's commission—the baptizing and teaching, the two great branches of the general design. These branches were to be determined by circumstances, which made it necessary to baptize Jews, Gentiles, and heathens teaching them Christ commission to discipline their children. Nevertheless, Jewish children of all ages were circumcised and then taught to do all that God had commanded them. But circumcision provided only a cleaner penis, after the foreskin was cut away, biblically circumcision did nothing. However, teaching baptism cleanses the soul while making ready for the acceptance of the Spirit of God through belief and trust.

There are several things to be noticed:

- The Lord seeks a universal empire and sends forth His armies to conquer the world. Every church and every disciple must understand that they have marching orders.

- Every saint is commanded to take steps to move the gospel forward, making disciples of students, other teachers, and scholars of Christ—not great philosophers, but babes in Christ Jesus who have entered the school of Christ and are taught afterward.

- This is for all nations—not just Jewish communities! In the Great Commission, Jesus looks beyond Judea and commands that the gospel be offered to all nations. The test of eighteen centuries shows that Christianity is not local or national but is adapted to the needs of all mankind. Christ came to be the Savior of the world, and His is a universal religion.

- How should disciples be made? By baptizing them in the name of the Father, Son, and Holy Spirit. Through baptism, those who believe are formally enlisted and enrolled in the school of Christ. Relative to the baptism of the Holy Spirit, the school of Christ includes those whom the Holy Spirit commands to minister to others in spirit and truth. Jesus alone was baptized with the Spirit; His apostles and disciples were baptized in water, so they baptized in water, and it is to this rite that He refers. When we turn to the preaching of the apostles under this commission, we find that all who were brought over unto one belief were at once baptized.

- Converts were to be baptized in the name of the Father, Son, and Holy Spirit. It is a positive affirmation of the Old Testament that where the name of the Lord is recorded, there will the Lord be present and meet His disciples. The Lord declares that the three names—Father, Son, and Holy Spirit—are recorded in baptism. The Father receives him as a child, the Son welcomes him as a brother, and the Holy Spirit endows him with that spirit by which he can say, "Abba, Father."

A pastor, the pastor's wife, an associate minister, a deacon, and a church member were engaged in Sunday morning studies. The study book called for an answer to three study questions:

1. How can you apply this lesson to improve our discipleship?
2. How can you use it to help someone who is struggling with learning to trust God?
3. Spiritually, what similarities do you see between yourself and Isaiah?

The second question became the focus of the study. To answer the second question, the pastor described this scenario:

A patient is about to be taken to surgery, but he's afraid of all the possibilities that could go wrong. One was the anesthetist might administer too much anesthesia, and the patient may not wake up. The doctor could make a fatal mistake, and the patient might die. During the procedure, the patient might suffer an adverse reaction that'll kill him. The patient was adamantly afraid of death.

The complexity of the question is that the patient struggles with trusting God he might not wake up. The pastor question to the members is; how would the members of the study group help the struggling patient to trust God?

The deacon said that he would quote scripture, but beyond that, he didn't know. The pastor's wife began preaching scripture as if she was in a pulpit. The pastor said, softly but sternly, "I wouldn't want anybody to preach to me if I was afraid of dying during surgery," and the group members somberly agreed with him.

The associate minister said, "I'd tell him the truth about what God said about fear, life, and death."

The pastor replied to the associate minister, "That sounds like you're going to send him off prepared for death, but what if he doesn't wake up? What if he doesn't know anything about God or the Bible."

For a moment, the associate minister sat quietly searching for an answer, and finally he said, "I don't know what I'd say."

The discussion focused on the third question. In discussing the third question, everyone except the associate minister expressed their humanitarian similarities to Isaiah. But they weren't sure about comparing themselves with Isaiah, "spiritually;" the question asked, "Spiritually, what similarities do you see between yourself and Isaiah?"

The Bible say – Isaiah 6:8 Also I heard the voice of the Lord, saying, Whom shall I send, and who will go for us? Then said I, Here am I; send me.

The Sunday school participants apparently did not investigate completely the third question. Isaiah had experienced a personal and intimate encounter with the Lord and had been born again, converted from carnal minded to spiritual minded. His call to prophesy, in the year when King Uzziah died, came with an awe-inspiring vision, encompassing a majestic visit and conversation with God.

Uzziah was one of four kings who reigned during the time of Isaiah's writings. The holiness of the scene with the Lord "sitting on a throne, high and lifted up, and the train of his robe filling the temple," (Isaiah 6:1) seeing and hearing the seraphim (angels) respond by attempting to cover themselves while simultaneously praising God, forced Isaiah to see himself in a different light. The shaking doorposts and smoke-filled house reverberated with signs of God's power and holiness.

Isaiah responded as God wants all people to respond. *Woe* refers to sorrow or grief. Seeing himself in the light of God's holiness convicted Isaiah of his sinfulness and inability to ever reach a comparable level of holiness. Isaiah's woefulness was highlighted by fear that having seen the King, the Lord of Hosts, would result in death for him.

We see inferences to the demise of the old Isaiah. Faced with grief over his sinfulness, Isaiah confessed his own sinfulness and acknowledged his existence among sinful people. As Isaiah totally surrendered himself to God, an angel touched Isaiah's lips with a burning coal and pronounced not only forgiveness, but also the expurgation of his sins. Being in the presence of Almighty God, however, caused Isaiah's experience to be much more revelatory and instructive about God's calls and expectations.

God wants us to speak the truth in Christ, which means to focus on Jesus and what He came to do. We are never to lie or put our own spin on the truth. Neither are we to try to market God's truth so that it will be more palatable in our culture. We are called on to speak the truth with no reticence or hint of deception, and God's Holy Spirit implants within us the power to do just that. There will be times when the message we have to share will not be well received by those who hear it. But we must speak out and live out what we believe, even when faced with intense pressure to remain silent.

It's important that we speak the truth from the proper motivation; our hearts must be filled with understanding for those who are lost. We are all called to live out the truth that we speak. If you are convinced that you are a guide for the blind, a light for those who are in the dark, an instructor of the foolish, and a teacher for infants, because you have in the law the embodiment of knowledge and truth—then why, you who teach others, do you not teach yourself? You who preach against stealing, do you steal?

God instills within us the power to sail straight into the face of the disaster. No matter what the obstacle, God always has an overriding purpose, and it is always for our best. We can conclude that going through a disaster is evidence that God loves us and that He is at work in our lives to produce perseverance, character, and hope as we share in our Lord's sufferings.

Allegiance to prayer, Bible study, and daily convictions help us see ourselves as God sees us. We should pray for God to reveal our sinfulness so that we can repent and change our ways. Christians should always pray and ask God for direction. Promotions come not from the east, west, north, or south but of God through obedience. God is the judge. He put down one and set up another. God determined what Isaiah needed in order to carry out His mission, and we must allow God to do the same for us. Imagine the confidence Isaiah must have felt when he could answer, "Here am I. Send me!"

The associate minister's intimate relationship with God abounded, and the Holy Spirit prompted him to answer the question pertaining to the struggling person's fear: "Tell him the truth." Prayer is not a one-sided conversation, nor is the conversation the minister would have with the struggling person. Build God's Word precept upon precept, and the truth will prevail as the Spirit of God boosts the person's faith. It's not for the minister to sing his own praises but to glorify God, because He's all powerful, forever present, and everywhere at the same time.

In time, night is almost gone, and the day is at hand. To be carnally minded is death, but to be spiritually minded is life and peace. The carnal mind is in opposition to God and cannot understand the things of God, for it is not subject to the law of God, so those who are in the flesh cannot please God. Therefore make no provision for the flesh; instead, make provisions to go into God's presence, putting Christ first in your life.

The old self becomes worn out, useless, and unconverted with a sinful nature. I must own the part of me that was rebellious against God and insubordinate to God's grace. I am blind to God's glory and unbelieving toward His promises. The term *old self* refers to a person before being converted and born again. The old self wants to remain corrupt with lust and deceit. Corruption occurs as a result of giving in to deceitfulness, evil cravings that are pleasant and promising in anticipation but hideous and disappointing in retrospect.

In this analogy, the old self is in Adam's clothes, and in Adam's clothes all shall die. If the old self isn't physically dead, then conversion has not occurred. This does not mean that the physical body is itself sinful, but that the body is an instrument that the power of sin uses to carry out its deeds of darkness, influence, and power over us. Flesh is a part of the believer that will remain unredeemed until we receive our glorified bodies. Then we will finally be free from the presence of sin, and the pleasure of sin will no longer possess our bodies.

"Ah, for a new man to arise in me,
That the man I am may cease to be!"

Alfred Lord Tennyson
Former Poet Laureate of the United Kingdom
https://en.wikipedia.org/wiki/Alfred

The flesh is that part of a believer that functions apart from and against the Spirit of God. Flesh stands against the work of the Spirit in the believer's new heart, because the flesh has desires. The unsaved person often never regrets the sinful things he does, because of personal satisfaction and lack of guilt and/or painful consequences. The sinful things he does, though often disappointing and disgusting to him, are nevertheless consistent with his basic nature. The old self has no internal conflict beyond whatever conscience may remain in his sinful state that satisfied a desire or an opportunity. Living with unredeemed human flesh creates great conflict with spiritual living, because of the message of the cross. Jesus shed his blood on the cross and died to sin so that we may have access to God. This seems like foolishness to people who are spiritually perishing every day and on their way to damnation, but to those of us who are being constantly saved, it is the power of God that's causing their transformation.

God never stopped speaking; people stop listening!

The old self was crucified with Jesus on the cross, and a new self has already arisen in us. We can confess that our sinful flesh has ceased to be, and we welcome the indwelling of the Holy Spirit into our new temples of God.

Because of the mystery of time, we need to get it right in this moment. We have brought ourselves to a state of peace and into a quiet dwelling in the Word of God. We have prayed, asking God to forgive us for being disobedient toward the Holy Spirit and to restore us to a right relationship with God. We've asked God to forgive us for the discomfort we've caused and for causing people to fall victim to Satan.

The father asked his son and his son's mother to forgive him. He rebukes Satan and now keep him under his feet, never allowing Satan to rise employing the Holy Spirit's help. The father consults the Holy Spirit and patiently waits for a response of either "No, not yet" or "Yes."

The old self is unregenerated—not part righteous and part sinful, but totally sinful. The old self is deprived of capacity and is without the slightest potential within himself to become unrighteous but righteousness prevailing and pleasing to God. The new self is regenerate, made pleasing to God through Jesus Christ, and the new nature is entirely godly and righteously guided by the Holy Spirit. The new self is not yet perfected or glorified, but is already spiritually alive, and holiness is at work in him. The new self will continue to grow in holiness, no matter how slowly or falteringly, because life grows by its very nature. The new self exhibits abundant strength to keep covenant with Christ.

This term *new self* describes our new position in Christ, which gives us new potential to practice daily the putting off of the filthy rags of darkness and putting on of righteous deeds of light by the power of the indwelling Holy Spirit. The new self is being re-created in the likeness of God's character. Those who confess Jesus Christ as Lord are faithful, like God! Peter says that we become "partakers of the divine nature (2 Peter 1:4)."

Many homeless shelters have a delousing room, where derelicts who have not had a bath in months discard all their old clothes and get thoroughly bathed and disinfected. The unsalvageable old clothes are burned, new clothes are issued, and the clean man emerges as a new creation. Then the Holy Spirit renews the mind, as the new man learns of Christ becoming lowly and charitable and knowing no fear.

That's a picture of salvation, except that in salvation, the new believer is given a completely new nature. The constant need of the Christian life is to keep discarding and burning the remnants of the old sinful clothing. The many *therefore* and *wherefores* in the New Testament usually introduce appeals for believers to live like the new creatures they are in Christ. Because of our new life, our new Lord, our new nature, and our new power, we are called to live a correspondingly new lifestyle.

There is no such thing as justification without sanctification. There is no such thing as divine life without divine living. The truly saved person lives a new and godly life in a new and godly realm. He lives now and forever in God's realm of grace and righteousness and can never again live in Satan's realm of self and sin. Just as the natural, sinful, unregenerate man cannot restrain the manifestation of what he is, neither can the regenerate man, he listens to the soft-spoken whisper of the Holy Spirit.

CHAPTER 8

Power by Faith in Love

Stagger not at the promises of unbelief.
Be strong in the faith.
Be fully persuaded that which God has promised,
He can perform.
He's faithful.
God is Love.

IT IS NOT ENOUGH TO defend the faith if we have not been transformed by the faith we defend. A follower of Christ is called to live a life that reflects this transformation, apart from ceremonial law but through the righteousness of faith. It is not through law that we receive God's promise, but through the righteousness that comes by faith. God's promises come by faith, so that it may be by grace that faith may be guaranteed to all. God gives life to the sick and spiritual dead, and He calls things that are not as though they are. Grace is an unmerited act of God's mercy, whereas faith is synonymous with belief; consequently, faith comes from hearing God's messages, and the messages are heard through the preached word of God and the teaching of Christ. Grace is what God gives us, and faith is a way of laying hold to it. Grace comes downward from God to us, and our faith reaches up to God.

The apostle Paul writes to the Hebrews concerning their faith. He starts his letter with the word *now*, which signifies "at this exact moment." Then comes the word *faith*. The word *now* illustrates the timing for the faith, which is immediate. *Now faith* means "at the present time" or "immediately" a person must believe God at His Word through doctrine and teachings. Then we must trust with confidence because He is obligated to His promises. Belief is not grounded on substantiation, but the substance of things hoped for! Hoping for things not seen at the moment manufactures faith and trusting that whatever is going to be received is predicated on the grace of God.

Hope is the feeling that what is desired can be obtained or that event will turn out for the better, but hope must be superseded by belief. That desire must be based on the methodology of God's Word through doctrine and teachings whatever is to come will come without a doubt because God said so. We often hope and wish for things despite not knowing how we might get them and without the knowledge of how the effects would effectually affect us and others. The quality or condition of what we want is not the matter of concern, it's the existence, it's the reality within the soul, an expectation of what is foreseen through the faithfulness of God. Faith proves to the mind the reality of things that cannot be seen by the eye nor imagined mentally which are supplied supernaturally by God.

There is a Study Bible, *The Knowing Jesus Study Bible*, (*The Holy Bible New International Version Copyright 1999, by the Zondervan Corporation*) begins Hebrews chapter 11 with the word "*Now*," and then it reads faith is guaranteed by the word *sure*—the surety of what is hoped for, having no doubt of a future state or an event will occur or happen although we cannot yet see it. Faith coupled with belief assures the promise of God protected by His divine character that He cannot lie.

Look at faith this way: The doctor says that a person has a malignant growth on his liver and that if it's not removed, he'll die. However, the growth is quite advanced, and other major organs have already been infected. The doctors are giving this man a 10 percent chance of coming out of the surgery alive, but if they don't do the surgery, there's a 100 percent chance that the man will be dead within a month. Here are the options: have the surgery and take a chance that it will be successful or do nothing and take a chance living beyond a month.

To do nothing is sure death, so the man decide to have the surgery. The doctors schedule the surgery for eight o'clock the next morning. That night the man calls his pastor, and the pastor bring the prayer warriors of the church and assemble in the hospital room. Through faith, they understand that worlds were framed by the Word of God, that things seen were not made of things that appeared.

The Spirit of God is present, because the prayer warriors have gathered in the name of Jesus. They pray by faith that the man is healed, cleansed of all unrighteousness, and is made whole in the name of Jesus. They ask humbly and earnestly of Jesus that all things be healed, and thanked Him, they believed healing had been done by faith before they left the man's room.

The next morning, the nurses came into the room to prep the man for surgery. They perform pre-operative test before surgery, extracted blood and other preliminary medical tasks. They took him to the surgery floor and continued pre-operational tasks. Surgeons came into the pre-op room and told him they needed more x-rays before the surgery due to some confusing results. Astonished at the results of the x-rays and blood work, they perform other tests and found no cancer. Befuddled, other specialists were summoned, and they all admitted being confused about the total absence of the cancer overnight.

This is why God tells us to pray for one another. The Spirit of God communicates with the spirit within man things that the flesh cannot comprehend, because the flesh lusts after things that can be seen. People who are after things of the flesh do mind the things of the flesh and are limited by what the flesh can and cannot accomplish, but people who are after the Spirit mind the things of the Spirit. In other words, those who are born of the flesh are worldly seekers who seek after tangible items they can see, and those who are born of the Spirit are spiritual. Spiritual seekers seek after godly directions for God's will to be done. The things God require of man can be learned wherefore the promises of God are added unto him. Those who walk in the light of the Spirit shall not fulfill the lust of the flesh. Tongue twister? Maybe but the truth is God does not lie and the flesh seekers can not understand the things of the spirit because of their belief.

Remember that in the beginning, God, who is Spirit, spoke man into existence as a spirit. That spirit is the spirit with whom God now communicate with that brought man into spiritual creation. That spirit can understand spiritual things. God created a physical man for that spirit and gave him life knowing His spirit would not always strive with man, because man is flesh. The flesh will die. Therefore, if we live after the flesh, we shall die spiritually also, but if we mortify the deeds of the body, we shall live spiritually now and into an eternal heaven.

The Holy Spirit helps us in our infirmities, while many times our infirmities are not readily known. For instance, we don't always know what we should pray. The Spirit makes intercession for us to the Father with groanings that cannot be uttered or understood. Christ suffered and died once and for all for sin, the just for the unjust, that He might bring us to God, He being put to death in the flesh, but quickened by the same Spirit that dwells within us. Therefore, there is now no condemnation for those who are in Christ Jesus, who walk not after the flesh but after the Spirit. Christ is with us in the Spirit with joy, seeing our events in time and the steadfastness of our faith in Christ.

The Spirit of the Lord shall rest upon us. The Lord's Spirit has esteemed us in wisdom and understanding, counsel and might, and in knowledge. There is no fear in love, for perfect love casts out fear. We who worship God in the spirit are the sons of God, and we rejoice in Christ Jesus and have no confidence in the flesh.

The options that the doctors gave in their report were based on what they had diagnosed. Their expectations were based on experiences that had taught them what's evident determined future outcomes relevant to what they had found. Based on the seriousness of the damage to the organs and the progressing nature of the cancer cells, the doctors had estimated when death would occur. However, faith in God is strong and unshakeable, despite the doctors' prognosis. Believing what God said, that a person in the body of Christ shall not die but live declaring the works of the Lord. God staggers not at the promise through unbelief. We must be strong in the faith, giving glory to God and being fully persuaded that what He has promised, He is able to perform.

We should always be confident knowing that while we are at home in the body, we are spiritually absent from the Lord. If then, we walk by faith and not by sight, we can be confident in God's Word in our willingness to be spiritually absent from the body to present with the Lord even if we die physically, it's spiritual gain. To see life spiritually through a spectrum that can't be imagined envisioning the plight is unspeakable. The direct observations give spiritual intellectual enlightenment and cause an outward physical change spreading abroad joy. The spiritual emotions are impressive to the mind leaving us speechless. No words can either explain or express the magnificent powerful act of this special sense into the foresight. The revelation, whether it's visual, a feeling, prophetic, or some other form of confirmation, the gloriousness of the rite is so overwhelming, we can only shake our heads and wave our hands. We can only give God the highest praise, shouting Hallelujah, and say thank you, Lord.

We must believe God for what we pray for that we will receive it.

But praying and not getting it does not mean God didn't hear us. God's will be His plan, our lives and our prayer maybe attached to somebody else and maybe to their detriment. Needless we shall pray. We are to ask God and it shall be given to us, to seek Him and we shall find Him, and to knock on the door to whatever is good and the door shall be opened to us. Be careful about nothing, don't be anxious for anything, but in everything by prayer and supplication with thanksgiving we are to make our requests known to God. The flesh profits a man nothing!

Our flesh desires what it sees, smells, touches, and hears that profits. So, be careful about nothing, and don't be anxious about anything. Instead of being anxious, just lay your case before God and trust Him to do all things well. If people are not gentle toward another on any account, they ought to appeal to God in prayer. Prayer is the outpouring of the soul while speaking humbly and earnestly giving thanksgiving as if God has already granted the request. After the prayer, the attitude is to wait for the request to come to fruition. We must always come to God not with a complaining spirit, but with a spirit of thankfulness for our present mercies.

Because of preposterous shame and distrustful modesty, some people stifle their desires as if they are either too small or too great, but this self-defeating behavior causes them pain and anguish. Who can pour you out with a free and filial confidence? God! It's not always proper to disclose desires to other people, who can and will pray against you and or think you're foolish. The surest mark of a soul free from care is self-esteem, wisdom, understanding, and the knowledge of God—all incorporated into prayer and joined with true resignation. Not being anxious is always followed by peace, which resonates in harmony with thanksgiving.

This strengthening aid at the end of the day removes the heavy load from our backs and enables us to sit and relax. Jesus carried the weight of humanity's sin on His back, but He removed this burden from us at the cross with His death, burial, and resurrection. His death met the demands of God's law that the slaughtering of animals for their blood to cover sin was indeed finished. Now we are called to hold unwavering hope in our profession of faith, never giving up on the daily physical and mental pain of our struggles toward the unforeseeable troubles of our responsibilities in life. We are to persevere, never giving up hope when life seem too difficult, and to encourage others to live characterized by love.

Faith!

A prominent business owner began losing sales, and soon he had to close the doors of his business for good. His wife took their two children and left him, and the bank foreclosed on their home. Then he became sick and spent his remaining savings on medication and doctor bills, and soon he was broke and homeless. He began begging, drinking cheap wine, and wandering the streets sleeping in doorways and on park benches. Wherever the evening caught him, that's where he slept. His neighbors watched him spiral downward to a degenerate state—unshaven, wearing the same smelly ragged clothes day after day, and carrying a wine bottle in his back pocket. The man was never sinful or disrespectful toward anybody, but when he'd try to talk to someone, they would shrug him off.

On Sundays, the man would stand outside the church and listen to the singing and preaching, then take a drink and wander on down the street. At least once during the week, he'd walk up to the church door and peek inside. Seeing nobody in the sanctuary, he'd go inside, kneel at the altar, and talk to God as if God was right there next to him.

One Wednesday, the pastor heard a man talking and came out of his study to see who it was. He saw the man on his knees, the palms of his hands together and up to his mouth engaged in earnest prayer. At the end of his prayer, the man thanked God for the present day then lifted the name of Jesus with praise and in adoration. When he finished, he got up and left. This kept up for three months every Wednesday and the pastor became accustomed to the visits. He'd stand off to one side of the sanctuary and listen while the homeless man talked to God.

One Wednesday, the pastor took his usual obscure position and waited for the man to come in, but the man didn't show up. For the next few days out of concern, the pastor asked about the man's whereabouts, then he learned that the man had died. The pastor immediately went to the funeral home and claimed the body. He made funeral arrangements and held the man's funeral in his church on a Saturday. About ten people showed up, and most of them were there because the pastor had spoken to them concerning the funeral and arranged the service. The pastor gave an amazing eulogy, testifying about the relationship the man had developed with God and he believed God had washed a sinful soul in preparation for His kingdom.

After the burial, the pastor's life was never the same. The pastor's heart had been transformed by witnessing the effects of God's power on a soul considered the least in society. His heart and mind had been pricked and transformed by the power of God's through the downtrodden man. His spirit underwent perfection building his most holy faith in God, realizing Jesus convicting sin, and giving power through love.

The words *born again* can mean a radical change of some kind, being born a second time, or being born from above. Jesus incorporated all three of these definitions. Spiritual rebirth entails being radically born a second time from above and according to Jesus, which is the only way into heaven. The Bible teaches that God offers us a brand-new start when we give our lives to Him. We are unable to be so diligent in following His commands that we can win His approval;

the only determining factor in our being made right with our God is the rebirth that He offers us through Jesus Christ, a transformation so revolutionary and radical that we can only be deemed a new creation.

The Word of God has the power to regenerate. But it's of God's own will and accordingly to His plan. He will bring us forth by His Word in truth, so that we and others might be a kind of first fruit of His creation. Being born again relates the Word of God to Christ being crucified and risen. In this position, we regard our mental conditioning to have been redirected from what we see to that which is to come. These circumstances are stored in our hearts and with meditation, education, and the Holy Spirit's help, we change. We look to God, and His Holy Spirit, who quickens our spirit, who will cause our new spirit to be enlivened and stimulated. Believing our rebirth within our hearts, and the work will be done unto us according to what God has willed for us. Like Nike, just do it; follow the will of God listening to our hearts without reservation or fear of challenges from outside influences, whether the assignments seem unrealistic or unfavorable. Do it as unto God.

A woman and her husband in their mid-sixties met a man online. This man was asking online if anyone had leftovers from Thanksgiving dinner that they'd be willing to share with him. The response was overwhelming, but not really helpful: "Don't you have relatives?" "I'll pray for you." "Can you ask your neighbors?" "I've got leftovers, but you'll have to come and get them." Some people talked among themselves about what a shame it was that the man didn't have Thanksgiving dinner.

However, the woman put together a hefty meal for two people that included enough food for two days, including sodas, cranberry sauce, gravy for the dressing, and even sweet potato pie. She wrapped up plastic silverware and napkins, then packed it all into bags and delivered it to the man. Upon her arrival, she learned that he was sick and lived in the basement. He had been in and out of the hospital, but out now because he needed to be home to take care of his very sick wife. She was confined to the bed. They had moved from another state, but sickness caused them to become dependent upon each other. The man thanked God in earnest for the meal, and they prayed prayers of thanksgiving together.

The human heart is the soil, you and I are sowers, and the Word of God is the seed that we plant in that soil. God quickens us unto obedience by His Holy Spirit and gives us the increase to carry out what it is He's to accomplish. The heart closes around the Word of God by faith, and the beginning of the new life is the product of living by hope within the expectation that what is not seen can be obtained at the will of God.

Faith comes from hearing the Word of God. Faith is the effect of a certain cause, and that cause is described in the Word of God. Repetition, study, and ministering have power to produce faith. We teach about believing, but we do not witness how to do so or give testimony about belief. The empowerment of the Holy Spirit teaches the biblical way and the intelligent way, as well as solidifying that God is real and true to His promises. When we're being led by the Spirit of God, we come to understand that some things are not for our good, but rather for the good of someone else. Giving up the natural life in exchange for a spiritual life with God is the ultimate goal of living. Is that hard to grasp? Dying naturally to be raised spiritually is gain, however we can die spiritually yet be alive physically. Dying spiritually can also be raised spiritually but by faith in the word of God and God. We are to tell people to believe in the word of God and give them something scriptural in which to believe, something for their faith to rest upon—saving faith.

Although the prominent business owner's plight turned deplorable, God still used him while at the same time the owner shouldered his ministry without knowing where it was going. God spoke into the man's heart and without question, and the man became obedient and began the journey that God had charted for him. As he was being led by the Holy Spirit and walking cautiously, prudently, and discreetly, the peace of God that surpasses all understanding came over this man and guarded his heart as he journeyed through the valley of the shadow of death. The demonic spirits that dwelled in those who had stolen from him and destroyed his family tried to destroy him and ultimately kill him. The man was alone, but he was not by himself and without knowledge and understanding of what tomorrow should bring. By faith, he steadfastly listened to his heart and continued to walk and not faint. God increased his strength and gave him power over the darkness and demonic spirits which plagued and complicated his life. His faith did not waver as he waited upon the Lord, even though humanity had abandoned him, and his struggles seem to increase daily. God faithfully gave him spiritual and physical strength to be mentally up spiritually and continue ministering as God ministered to him. The man walked in the light of God for it was this sight God directed him until he physically died.

In this busy world, our minds try to comprehend the things of God intellectually, but when God speaks into our heart, the mind can't conceive what the heart knows to do. God spoke through the tears and strife of the alcohol, depression, and rejection—and into this man's heart. Many times, God's grace and mercy saved this man's physical life, supplying him with comfort and spiritual protection. When his mind showed him because he had no money to buy food, he was not going to eat, God spoke into his heart and told him to stand on God's promise to provide thus the man ate. The man's mind couldn't rationalize that at first, but by his faith in God's Word, God delivered and sustained him—and he ate. Grace and mercy drew the man's spirit forefront and closer to God whereby he became one who kept company with God providing services unbeknown to him with passion arising from his relationship with God whom he knows supports him.

When a voice spoke within the man's mind telling him that he was all alone and nobody cared about him, which was the scenario he faced every day, the Spirit of God spoke into his heart. He was constantly reminded God was with him always.

"I am with you alway, even unto the end of the world" (*Matthew 28:20)*. God's word had been seeded in the man's heart in order for him to recognize them as the voice of God. When the Holy Spirit spoke with the still, small voice, His voice was recognized not pretentiously but faithfully. The man heard the Spirit of God and his faith in God became stronger.

Jesus taught His disciples in the presence of those who were sick and needed. The multitudes were receiving healings and deliverance from sin and sin nature and from worldly captivities and they were extraordinarily gratefully unto Him. The joy of Lord Jesus resonated deep down within the soul of man and constituted an unexplainable joy the world cannot give nor take away. The disciples learned this joyful attribution as servants to bring the children of God into the body of Christ.

King David preached lessons he had learned early and throughout his life during the Old Testament era. He knew God firmly fixed within his heart His presence and He would be with him and deliver him from Satan. The Word of God would be David's sword and shield as long as he maintained a righteous heart to keep his mind, teachings, and faith in God without doubting.

The New Testament era is now profoundly substantiated by the promised Messiah, Jesus. Jesus lived demonstrating God's will for man mandating stewardship to man for man and most importantly, the glory due unto God for His workmanship that do not rest with man. Man is rewarded accordingly as to how and what he teaches others or the lack there of and according to his obedience to God. Jesus know all that Father God has given Him and He has given all that He knows to the people who believe Him and these people, Jesus declares are His. These same people praise, honor, and admire Jesus because acquiring the knowledge of the Father, God, have assured them the knowledge to the mystery to living a spiritual life. Knowing God through learning and knowing the Holy Scriptures gives a Divine Revelation to the will of God for mankind and spiritually lead them to a heavenly life in the earth realm.

Those who would get true learning must get it out of the Scriptures. Those who speak revelations and teach do not speak from themselves but deliver what they have received from God. They know the scriptures are profitable for all purposes of Christian life and they are suitable for every case in life, teaching, correction, and reproving.

Scriptural teachings are for facilitating righteousness unto all through God's commandments. Those who diminish the value of the commandments shall be called the least in the kingdom of God and those who demonstrate the principle quality by showing life's natural character in itself shall be called great in the kingdom of heaven.

King David inclined his heart to believe the needy will be not forgotten and included himself within this group. He believed God's statues and performed them always as unto God until the end of his life. Jesus remarked this mindset as one that is poor true spirit that David life's work would be blessed toward perfection as God is perfect. The perfection of being poor in spirit is the journey back to God allowing God to sit on the throne of our heart and not being anxious for nothing;" (James 1:4) it is noble to be patient and allow God to work through us to obtain what it is He's accomplishing. This spirit is the kingdom of heaven.

The destitute man believed what God was saying, and by faith he was becoming one with God. He was still wearing the clothing—the sinful nature clothes of the first Adam, but he was shedding those clothes layer by layer as the light of God purified him. And as God promised, the man was loved, fed, clothed, sheltered, and never alone for the Spirit of God was with him.

God used the destitute man's situation to reach the pastor, who in turn reached others in truth. The man's plight became a testimonial tool to minister to the pastor, who witnessed the sincerity of the man's prayer within his heart and encompassed the Spirit of God, also God's peace, joy, and happiness. The pastor first handed witnessed God's restorative process at work as the man's faith became stronger. He witnessed the man becoming more and more intimate with God through belief and faith and his faithfulness by retuning to be spiritually fed. And as a result of the destitute man's dedication to God in spite of his earthly physical condition, the pastor's ministry became more viable through his understanding the mystery in the scriptures.

The pastor's teaching declared, with ceremony and authority, the unadulterated truth of the Word of God. He understood the true effect of teaching to love, preparing the congregation's hearts with capable seeds of the Word to receive and to do what the Lord requires of us all.

We should all call upon the Lord, and He will listen to us, but do we pray for what we want or what we need? Our needs are not always truly necessities, nor are they always good for us. We don't want to bring hurt or some sort of calamity upon ourselves or those closest to us. Do we know what we want or need? Why must we seek the Lord in order to find Him? Why should we search for Him with all our heart?

There's a man in his late seventies who respects his age and his own abilities, and he appreciates waking up every morning. When he first opens his eyes, he says, "Thank you, Lord." Then he sits on the side of the bed and pushes himself up to a standing position. He doesn't move until he's sure that his legs will bear his weight. Then he gingerly takes a few steps, making sure that his lower extremities are communicating with his brain and will support his upper body. Then he goes on about his day.

When we pray to God, God will put no more on us than we can bear, like the man who will not put more weight on his legs than they can bear. This analogy is true about God in every way when it comes to us because He knows everything about us – our past, present, and future. Remember, God know the plans He has for us in order to prosper us and not to harm us. His plans are to give us hope and a future therefore He knows before we ask for something, even when we ask for something we can't endure.

Sometimes God's answer is "Yes, and amen," but often times the answer may be "Not yet," because we might not be equipped or prepared to receive the gift for which we're asking. If the thing we're asking for would bring harm to ourselves or someone else,

God's answer is no. Because at the present, we don't possess the proper spiritual attitude, even though we may not understand why, God does. God may put us on a spiritual road of preparation for the transformation to receive that particular desire, so we need to be vigilant, watchful, alert, and aware of His arming. We must become steadfast and unmovable in the precepts of the Word of God, through study and revelations, ready for the spiritual battles with Satan, who wants us to fail physically and spiritually.

If we're flesh minded and fight against the spiritual transformation by not accepting the guidance of the spirit of truth, then we will not receive the increase we pray for. God's plan is not to hurt us or allow us to hurt others, but for us to prosper by faith in love as we willingly surrender to Him and adopt His right way to prosper others. God has a will for our lives, and we have a will of our own, but in surrendering our will, we put our will inside His and then follow God's way to obtain His will then our will, will be met. Our will must be in line with what God has said concerning us, therefore we must study our Bible to be clear for oneself what God has said. We are individuals each having a view of life as we see it and experienced it. Our independent assessment of life has been influenced by what has happened, cause and effect, and perceptions all have shaped emotions and views. Nevertheless, our lives ought to be predicated on scriptures not on another person perceptions or beliefs, thus scripture deal in individuality building acceptance and belief of His word.

Therefore, we must ask of our desires in faith and then allow the Spirit of God to govern our personal being speaking into our hearts. The heart knows what the mind cannot understand because it's busy trying to figure out logically what God is saying. This intellectual struggle is common within us and there is nothing wrong with it, but God's Spirit requires the mind (flesh) to step aside so that the heart can adhere to the voice of the Lord.

We're required to obey the Spirit's instructions to build faith, trust and a God-like character. Obedience and trusting the actions of the Holy Spirit is of the utmost importance to our spiritual transformation. As a renewed person, we are better able to manage what God has for us. Though it may not be what we prayed for, it might be a better, a more perfect gift.

How important is belief for faith? We have the captured, restored, transcribed writings of God collected in the Bible. Included are stories by chosen writers inspired by God revealing extraordinary episodes in their lives. These writers experienced things almost beyond belief, but the events happened and are recorded for us. The people God chose were not the bravest, smartest, healthiest, or fittest; they were irregular, deviant, and malformed. But through their phenomenal, extraordinary, astounding, amazing, and remarkable feats and realizations, these people were shown to believe God. This select group of people preached what God made known to each one of them, that He was real. He revealed His purpose through His promises, and yet many of people did not believe in the living God. They fought against the preaching and rejected the teaching, denying the living God and godliness.

The Old Testament period was chaotic with unbelief, unfaithfulness, sin, and shame. During the intertestamental period, there were no prophets or messages from God, only a seemingly endless void after the prophet Malachi. Some people assumed that God had forgotten them, and others concluded that He no longer cared. During this time of unrest and change, traditional power blocs were realigned and a Near Eastern cultural tradition that had been dominant for almost three thousand years passed away. The intertestamental years were anything but silent, as events, literature, and social forces shaped the world laying the groundwork for the New Testament. From the very beginning, Jesus is pictured as the One who fulfils the prophecies of the Messiah, and His arrival changed the course of history.

Jesus's ministry was characterized by the announcement of a new covenant with God, not as a repudiation of the old covenant, but as a final fulfillment of it. God prepared the Jewish people to look for the One whom the prophets had promised. However, God was preparing the Jewish and Gentile people alike to receive the good news of His grace in Jesus Christ. The unity of the testaments points to the same God, the same theology, and the same divine promises. The Christian faith is an expression of confidence in those promises, the belief that Jesus is indeed the Son of God, the promised Messiah, the Savior and Redeemer of humankind. The Son of God was the One about whom all the prophets testified.

The New Testament supplies four portraits of the same person in the Gospels, and the themes and structures of the four Gospels are all different. The men who wrote these accounts were convinced that these events were distinctive and separate, although part of a larger series. They witnessed Jesus's impressive spiritual acts of achievement. The Gospels overflow with confidence that in all four portraits, Jesus was indeed the Savior, God's promised One:

Gospel	Portrait	Characteristic
Matthew	King	Royalty
Mark	Servant	Ministry
Luke	Son of Man	Humanity
John	Son of God	Deity

The New Testament completes the picture of Jesus Christ, who was introduced in the prophecies and foreshadowed in the figurative language of the Old Testament.

Biblical terms such as *Messiah, Redeemer, Shepherd, Son of Man,* and *Son of David* originated in the Old Testament and find their ultimate significance in the New Testament. The biblical picture of Jesus unfolds in each section of the New Testament.

<u>Gospels</u>	Manifestation of Jesus
<u>Acts</u>	Propagation of the good news of Jesus
<u>Epistles</u>	Explanation of Jesus
<u>Revelation</u>	Consummation of Jesus

The more closely we examine the person, character, and claims of Jesus, the more we will be compelled to see that He was more than just a man. A mere man who said the sort of things Jesus said would not be a great moral teacher. He would either be a lunatic, on the same level as a man who says he is a poached egg, or the devil himself. This man was—and still is—either the Son of God, a madman, or worse. The claims of Jesus are so startling that they stop us in our tracks and challenge us to make up our minds about this most remarkable person. Was He just a great teacher, or was He something more?

Jesus was born in obscurity, raised in poverty, and crucified in deep personal humiliation and disgrace. Yet He transformed the ancient world and continues to transform lives today. Those who put their faith in Him find Him to be more than enough to meet their deepest needs.

There is a certain wholeness about the Jesus who preached the arrival of the kingdom of God, who ate with corrupt tax collectors and sinners, who healed the sick and raised the dead, who died on the cross and rose triumphantly from the dead. Attempts to strip the supernatural from Jesus's life can only produce a Jesus so radically different that He is unrecognizable and His effect on history unexplainable. You may have developed a contrary belief, but Jesus is a greater Savior than you think Him to be, even when your thoughts are at their highest or lowest.

Jesus's sayings and teachings were so extraordinarily wise that many people view Him as a great teacher. He championed the cause of oppression and offered freedom, confounding the religious and social establishments of His day. Some people saw Him as a social revolutionary. He touched those who suffered from leprosy, healed the sick, and raised the dead, and many people remember Him as a great healer. Because His life serves as a model for leadership development, some people envision Him as the ultimate corporate leader, the perfect CEO.

Jesus is so much more, and as we introduce Him as our Lord to others within the modern context, we may be in danger of missing the purpose of His life. An angel directed Joseph to name Mary's infant son – *Jesus*, meaning "the Lord saves," because He would save His people (the people who believed Him to be the Messiah) from their sins. To understand this is to understand why our Savior came. We must have a realistic understanding of the human condition.

From early on, Jesus's life was fueled by compassion, love, and vitality. Every event was surrounded by the spirit of darkness, exposing Jesus to every feeling that exists within humanity. It was important that He experience the weight of them, but what was more important was how He overcame the spirit of darkness with the power of love.

God is love, but have we loved God? He undoubtably loves us. God sent His Son, Jesus, to regain our love and supply instructions for His favor in exchange for our sin. If God so loved us, why shouldn't we also love one another? We have never seen God, yet we say we love Him, but we live among one another and show little to no love at all for one another. God dwells in us and His love is perfected in us through the Holy Spirit but still we don't love each other. If we do not believe that we dwell in God, and God in us, and that God has given us His Spirit, then Jesus's life, death on the cross, and resurrection have no real value. Where is the power in love? Jesus mantle was an indication of His authority and responsibility as God's chosen spokesman to us to have a bold and tenacious faith that will not let go of God. Through Jesus, God demonstrated to us that His love for us was so great, He gave His only begotten Son's life as a ransom for our righteousness. We are to love one another while remaining unmoved by circumstances, persevering against evil, being persistent until we see the full restoration of the power of the ministry of Jesus in our midst. The same Holy Spirit which raised Jesus from the dead is the same Holy Spirit that will lead us back to God. That same Holy Spirit that was poured out then is available today. God has not changed. The Holy Spirit has not changed.

Those who believe God have seen and do testify that the Father sent the Son to be the Savior of the world. God loves anyone who confesses that Jesus is His Son and God will dwell in them, and they dwell in God, thus they have known and believed the love God has for us. Here is where love is made perfect, that we may have the boldness in the day of judgment, because as God is in the world, so are we.

We ought to love God, because He first loved us. For us to

show we possess love for God is to speak and do as He do. How can we hate our brother with whom we interact with every day, and yet say we love God whom we've never seen? Can we operate in faith without human emotions, remembering God is faithful to humanity? God commands that we love one another because we love Him, then we must love our brother.

John the Baptist, a servant of Jesus was sanctified by God and preserved to pave the way for Jesus. John the Baptist lived a low-quality lifestyle in the desert, the wilderness, eating locusts and wild honey, while preaching a strange message. Unlike so many people, he knew his mission in life and accepted it. He clearly understood that he had been set apart by God for a purpose.

Through God's direction, John the Baptist challenged people to prepare for the coming of the Messiah. He taught the people to turn away from sin and baptized them as a symbol of repentance and acceptance to what was before them. Although he held no power of influence in the Jewish political system, he delivered his message with the force of authority. People could not resist the overpowering truth of his words as they flocked by the hundreds to hear him and be baptized. And even as he attracted the attention of the crowds, he never lost sight of his mission—to steer people to Christ.

In approximately 29 AD, Herod Antipas had John the Baptist arrested and put in prison. Later John was beheaded through a plot devised by Herodias, the illegal wife of Herod and ex-wife of his brother, Philip. John the Baptist ministry was a remarkable one which included the Baptism of Jesus in the Jordan River. John's greatest strength was his focused and faithful commitment to the call of God on his life.

Jesus declared John the Baptist to be the greatest man to

have ever lived. Taking the Nazirite vow for life, John the Baptist personified the term *set apart for God*. John knew that he had been given a specific job to do, and he set out with singular obedience to fulfill that mission. He didn't just talk about the repentance of sin, he personified that quality with boldness of purpose throughout his uncompromising mission. He was willing to die a martyr for his stand against sin. John the Baptist did not set out with the goal of being different from everyone else. Although he was remarkably strange, he wasn't merely aiming at uniqueness. Rather, he targeted all his efforts toward obedience to God for the mandate on his life. Obviously, John hit the mark, as Jesus called him the greatest of men.

When we come to realize that God has given us a specific purpose for our lives, we can move forward with confidence, fully trusting the One who called us. Like John the Baptist, we don't have to fear living with a radical focus on our God-given mission.

Can there be any greater joy for man towards his fulfillment to God in this life than to know that God experiences pleasure that He empowered humanity to share true love with him. The ability to feel and experience the joy of God is a gift that come from God, truly there is no greater pleasure for God or man. Our chief end is simply to please God whereby in our pleasing Him, we inevitably will be pleased as well, and our reward awaits us in heaven. Undoubtedly, moments after John the Baptist beheading, he must have heard God say, "Well done!"

It does not matter how we die, but know we are going to die! Death simply enables the spirit to separate from the earthly body. What matters is what we do while we are alive—how we treat other people and spread pure love, unadulterated love that's not diluted or polluted by man's definitions. The enemy of life has diluted and polluted the statement, "I love you but I'm not in love with you." How can you love someone and not be in love with them? The carnal mind can answer this question with mental orientations with divisions in sexual connotations, but the Spirit of God sees no difference.

Don't be ashamed of the testimony of our Lord but be a partaker of the afflictions of the gospel according to the power of God. God has saved us and called us with a holy calling, not according to our works, but according to His own purpose and grace, which was given to us in Christ Jesus. God knew us before the world began. Because of our Lord and Savior Jesus Christ, He has abolished death and brought life and immortality to light through the gospel that we have power by faith, through Jesus. The gospel of Jesus is depicted in the first four books of the New Testament of the Bible.

God has not given us a spirit of fear but through Jesus, He has given us power through demonstrated love to having a sound mind. If we walk in the light of Jesus' authoritative command because He is in the light of the world, then we can have a true loving fellowship with one another. The blood Jesus shed on Golgotha, the place outside ancient Jerusalem where Jesus was crucified on the cross, cleanses us from all sin. If we say that we have no sin, we deceive ourselves and the truth is not in us that's because we have sinful natures. But if we confess our sins to God and one to another and ask to be forgiven, God *is* faithful and just to forgive us of our sins and cleanse us from all unrighteousness. That is true love. We are to renew our minds based on truth which prove the goodness, the acceptable and the perfection in God. This is the greatest pleasure for

God and man that we do not conform to the world but transform our minds by the will of God.

Satan has mechanisms that attract our eyes, nose, and ears through emotions that trigger desires and feelings. This mechanism of attraction plays into our innate character without our conscious knowledge of being manipulated, and then we fall into position for the attack Satan has planned. We become yoked with him.

A yoke is a wooden frame, consisting of a bar with an oxbow, a U-shaped frame forming a collar about an ox's neck holding the yoke in place and use for attaching the necks of a pair of animals, such as oxen, so that they can be worked as a team. The spirit of Satan and the Spirit of God cannot occupy the same yoke. Our bodies are temples of God, and God and Satan cannot occupy the same temple. We determine who occupies our temple, God or Satan. We determine whether we follow God or Satan, by our deeds honoring one or the other—but not both.

What does someone who believes Jesus is the Son of God have in common with a nonbeliever? Eventually one will persuade the other to believe as they do. If they don't work together, they will pull against each other. There will be chaos, and they both will be miserable. Thus, Satan has won because misery is his goal! Let's not be unequally yoked with unbelievers, for what fellowship has righteousness with unrighteousness? What communion does light have with darkness except but to lead one out.? Come out from among them, be separate, don't touch unclean things, and Jesus will receive you. The word unclean means everything the word of God says unclean is. Let's stick to the Bible and don't try to find reasons for not obeying the word of God.

Making an indirect reference to a command and principle to

make a point though, the language is indeed greater than it really is but the point is clear. The Church is to make zero association with sinners except acting to win over souls for Christ. Concerning discipline, if anyone does not recognize this, they are not recognized and there is nothing unique or strange in such instructions. The Old and New Testaments produce perfect harmony with no contradictions in God's word, the text simply means we should not touch anything which is unclean.

Jesus told people to take His yoke and learn about him. He is meek and lowly in heart, and we will find rest for our souls. His yoke is easy, and His burden is light. He said if those of us who labor and are heavily loaded with deep painful feelings should come to Him, He will give us rest.

With Jesus, the blind receives their sight, the lame walk, the lepers are cleansed, the deaf hear, the dead are given life, and the poor in heart have the gospel preached to them. People who refused to see the goodness of our Lord can now see, lame people now are walking and diseased people cleansed of their sickness. People who couldn't hear the Spirit of the Lord now can hear Him speak into their hearts, all through the power of God.

Being yoked with Jesus by an indwelling of the Holy Spirit can defeat the devil. The fight is not ours, but the Lord's; the fight belongs to God through Jesus. When Jesus ascended into heaven and sat at God's right hand, the Holy Spirit was released onto earth's atmosphere. The Holy Spirit is like the wind, for you can't tell where it came from or where it's going, but you know it's there. We are fortunate that we didn't exist before Jesus fortunately, the Holy Spirit enabled believers to trust God, live holy lives, and serve the Lord in power. The Spirit of God was known to those to whom He chose to present Himself to, and others had to believe what the bearer of the manifestation told them. During their time, the bearer of God's divine message spiritually saw what was to happen by revelation, and their faith was made sure by the power and evidence of His Word coming to fruition. Jesus's death, burial, resurrection, and ascension were compelling evidence that solidified Jesus as the Son and Word of God.

Jesus's death on the cross made it possible for the Spirit of God to come to earth and do God's work. That same Spirit of God that raised Jesus from the dead dwells in us. He who raised up Jesus shall also revive life in us and cause us to become alive—receive eternal life, restore lost souls, stir life in the dying, evangelize, visit the sick and shut in, feed the hungry, and stimulate our mortal bodies through fellowship. This is all possible because of the Holy Spirit inside us.

We must know that we dwell in God and He in us, because He has given us His Spirit. We must know that our bodies are the temple of the Holy Spirit, and thus we are not our own.

We must be intimate with God through Jesus by the Holy Spirit, who helps us through to obedience and faithfulness. We must study the Bible and learn from the teachings the substance of things hoped for and the evidence of things not seen, to build our faith to transform our character unto the likeness of God. As it is written, then we can call those things that are not as though they are.

Studying the Bible gives us tools to keep Satan out of our temples. God has a covenant agreement with us now that we are temples of the living God. He will live and walk with us as our God, and we will be His people. Jesus gave us two great commandments: We must love God with our hearts, souls, and minds, and we must love our neighbors as ourselves. All the commandments of God hang on these two. Holding true to these commandments empowers us to keep Satan under our feet by faith in the Word of God.

The power in our faith is released through the love of God by our belief and trust. Through faith, we understand that worlds were framed by the Word of God, so that what is seen has not been made from things which are visible. Believing that God will do what He says is the power, the ammunition for waging warfare with unclean spirits and degenerate powers. God's Spirit dwells within us, so we're empowered spiritually, therefore we must be spirit minded. We must trust this power that rests within us because it bestows upon us the victory over Satan every time. Therefore, we walk as if Satan has already been defeated by faith.

By faith, Abel offered God a better sacrifice than Cain. Because of his obedience and faithfulness, he was commended as a righteous man. God spoke well of his offering. And as a result of his obedience and faithfulness, Abel still speaks into the hearts of many people, even though he is dead.

Enoch was taken from this life, so that he did not experience a physical death. Before he was taken, he was commended as one who pleased God. Without faith, it's impossible to please God, because anyone who comes to God must believe that God exists and rewards those who earnestly seek Him.

When called to go to a place where later he would receive his inheritance, by faith, Abraham obeyed and went, even though he did not know where he was going. By faith, Abraham made his home in the promised land like a stranger in a foreign country. A stranger in a foreign country who has lost his memory to the only country he knows and searches for clues to his identity without success.

Abraham is compelled to build a new life to find himself and God to discover his new identity to navigate through life with God's counsel before everything is lost.

Nevertheless, the old, familiar, and forgotten come looking for him and tries to recover under the spirit of Satan to come crashing in on him. This attention will cause trouble and the new person need God not to find the old self but to continue course to renewal. Abraham lived in tents, as did Isaac and Jacob, who were heirs with him of the same promise, for he looked forward to the city whose architect and builder is God.

God renewed His covenant with Abraham. Abraham and his wife, Sarah, were both well up in age, well past the age to have children, and yet a child was born. Their son, Isaac, established the lineage leading to the birth of Jesus, and this same covenant established God's faithfulness towards all people of faith. This Abrahamic covenant is an everlasting covenant which extends into the future of Christians. We are blessed to take part in the same covenant blessings as Abraham. The Prophet Ezekiel prophesied a day when Israel would be fully restored to the promised land as a nation. Israel will be blessed and redeemed as God promised.

When people challenge our faith, we can ask the Holy Spirit to move in their lives so that they too may respond gratefully to God's love and humbly accept His forgiveness. We don't have to worry that Satan, God's enemy, will defeat us with his schemes. When they hurled insults at Jesus, He didn't retaliate, even though He suffered at the people hands He came to deliver. Instead, He entrusted Himself to His Father, God, who judges everyone justly. Jesus bore our sins in His body on the tree, so that we might die to sin and live for righteousness, for by His wounds we have been healed of all degradation and sin.

As a man, Jesus was indeed finished after He took his last breath. His death consummated a process that God had begun at the beginning of time. The Old Testament prophecies concerning the Messiah's sufferings had been fulfilled, and every provision necessary for our salvation from sin was in place.

The fact that God's plan of salvation is so exclusive shapes how we as His children are called to set our priorities. We cannot ignore the plight of family and friends who do not know Jesus. There may well be people in our neighborhoods who have virtually no interest in Jesus, whereby God will send us to them to adapt them to Jesus the Savior. We may even be called to travel to a foreign country to share the good news with people who may not have heard of Jesus or of a way to find life in Him. Each day, as we rub shoulders with those around us, we should ask ourselves this question: "What can I do right now to get the message to this person who needs to know Jesus?"

One of the most difficult things for us to learn is to focus on Jesus. We are encumbered by earthly cares that urgently press for attention without maintaining a sense of perspective, we can all too easily succumb to the cruel and oppressive rule of the urgent that we slip into thinking that these immediate concerns matter most. Our real challenge, however, is to fix our eyes on Jesus. *Fix* means to deliberately set aside time and to concentrate in stillness with determination and commitment. To fix our gaze on Jesus, we need a deep longing to know Him, coupled with a genuine willingness to devote time to Him alone.

Our celestial bodies are composed of many distinct parts, some of which can operate independently of others; nevertheless, collectively our body parts depend on each other. The collection of our bodies into one whole, is also coordinated, blending into a functioning and unified whole allowing all types of people to be included and participate. We are individuals who don't need anybody's external additions for life. We do need each other's physical assistance to survive, but our very existence is influenced by others through trust, energy, knowledge, finances, touch, smell, emotions, and so on.

As we approach the end of our lifetime on the road to eternity, the Lord has not changed His commitment to His purpose. He's committed by covenant to save people and to seek out and forgive those whom the self-righteous leaders have condemned. Jesus came to show us what God is like, to help us understand God, and to bring us back to Him. We could never do this by ourselves, so we must uphold our end of the covenant. There is a right way to obey God, and Jesus established the methodology for always doing it the right way. Jesus chose to suffer and die so that we might live physically and spiritually. Every Christian is called to do the works that Jesus did, so that everyone may choose to live.

A Nurse's Story

The young man's knee hurt so much that it felt like bone rubbing against bone. At his wife's suggestion, they went to a medical facility for a diagnosis and pain medication. X-rays revealed that he had arthritis, which had inflamed his knee joint. The doctor ordered a knee brace and a shot in the hip. A nurse came into the examining room to administer the shot, bringing with her the syringe and medication. While she prepped the area on the man's upper hip for the injection, fear came over the young man about the needle stick. The nurse observed the obvious attitude change and began to engage him in a jovial conversation. The young man began relaxing more and more while his wife joined in filling the atmosphere with bright spirits. The nurse talked while she injected the medication, and the wife gave a motivational talk branding the man to to be stern in stature but good-humored with the nurse.

During the conversation, the nurse told the couple that in a single year, she had been involved in multiple automobile accidents and lost her son to death. As she mentioned the tragedy, her mood became much darker, gloomy, and her voice revealed a strong inner compulsion to express something truly deeper and intimate. She lowered her voice almost to a whisper and her eyes filled with tears. Asking their pardon for her somber behavior, she shared her story with them.

She began her story by telling the man and his wife she had been experiencing depression and had feared for her son's life. To protect him, she had moved her family from a crime-infested part of the county to a safer, more upscale neighborhood. Her son, the oldest of three children, had always looked out for his two younger sisters taking a father role in their lives.

In the new neighborhood, the nurse had begun looking for a church home for the children. After visiting various churches, the children decided they liked one particular church, so they secured their fellowship there, joining and soon became instruments in the church serving God.

One night her son came home from work, the nurse looked at him and saw something peculiar. She had no idea what it was, but she had a feeling God was trying to tell her something. Her son was a good role model for his sisters. He earned good grades in school, enjoyed playing sports, worked a part-time job, and owned his own car. His mother couldn't figure out what the unfamiliarity was, that strangeness without a known parallel. He possessed a pleasant oddness about him. She called her mother and talked with her about him. Her mother couldn't tell her anything specific, but she told her daughter to pray.

The nurse had called her ex-husband and told him that she had seen something unexplainable on their son. She felt compelled to tell the boy's father that he needed to spend more time with the son. The father took offense. Being out of their lives, now suddenly, she's asking him to step up into his father role to interact with their son. His involvement with his children had always been limited, and though she pleaded with him to reach out more, he ignored the matter. To her this matter implied an imposing self-consciousness of importance to reach a state of acceptance into something of a higher worth.

Not many days afterward, the nurse was awakened by a phone call late one night. Her son was driving home from work when his car struck a concrete highway divider. The nurse rushed to the hospital, only to find out her son died in the crash.

Devastated by the death of her son, the nurse had slipped into depression. The depression was a factor in her three automobile accidents over the last year. She asked herself if she had done all she could to keep her son safe and steer him toward God? She sought out answers from people whom she trusted, but that only drove her into deeper levels of mental confusion. She mentally withdrew affectionately from family. She stopped socializing with friends secluding herself in her home.

Her daughters seeing their mother's behavior began to affect them emotionally, they took on the role of her comforters. Their attachment to their mother and God had proven worthy. They did not understand losing a child after trying to protect him from worldly dangers then lose him to an incident she had no control. This was extremely hard on their mother. But to know that our lives are God's business, the daughters ministered to their mother what they knew about God. The ministry of the daughters proved beneficial because the nurse slowly awakened to understand that although her son had been a joy she shared with her daughters, God is greater.

She began meditating on Jesus. Through her meditation, she realized she needed to go on living for her daughters. So, she focused on doing well at her job, particularly with regard to the well-being of her patients, their happiness, and their successful recovery.

The daily concerns and pressures of life do demand our attention. A loving fixation on someone we can't see is a continuous challenge, so we need to rely on trust and faith. What makes this mindset possible? Does having faith mean having confidence in both what we hope for and what we do not see?

The nurse had not been able to realize God's plan. If she had, she would never have gone along with it. Her love for her children had driven her to finish nursing school, earn her degree in nursing, get a good well-paying job to support them, and steer them toward God. That was the nurse's plan, and she had not reached the end, yet her conscious impulse was to keep on walking, marching steadily and laboriously for the welfare of her children. She understood the walk was long and tiring and it was a slow march, heavily burdened but more was to come, so she took a deep breath and girded her strength and continued in her struggle to make her plan happen. But God has a plan too.

Still, almost a year later after her son's death, an older man showed up at the medical facility where the nurse worked. He had stubbed his big toe and was in pain. He and the nurse was engaged in conversation about his toe when they began talking about how great God is. Significantly moved by the conversation, the man began telling the nurse his testimony.

He had suffered from a bad heart. The doctors told him that he would die soon because of his heart failing condition. He became a recipient for a heart transplant and was put on the list awaiting a heart but now one was not available. His conditioned worsened so he and family members were prepared for him to die. One night, however, he was informed that a heart had become available. Right then and there, the man thanked God and praised Him for saving his life.

Talking with the nurse, the man told her that a young man had crashed his car into a concrete pillar and died. The young man's mother donated her son's heart, and because of that mother, he was alive today. The man told the nurse that six other people had received organ donations from that young man—his eyes, lungs, kidneys, liver, pancreas, and intestines, all had given new life to people who desperately needed them. As the nurse and the old man talked more about the accident and the young man's death, she realized that it was her son who had made that difference. Later she contacted her transplant coordinator, who confirmed that the heart of that nurse's son was truly beating inside her patient's chest.

When we stop concentrating on experiencing the pleasures of this life and develop a singular focus on Jesus, we learn that He is indeed the author and perfecter of our faith. Our faith strengthens us even when we are corrected and disciplined by our loving Father, as we learn to live a life that pleases Him. If we train our thoughts on Jesus, He promises to come to our aid when we are weary and tempted to give up.

The nurse was thrilled to have given birth to a child whose life made a difference in the lives to seven other people. She thanked God for not taking a life, but instead allowing others to live.

As the nurse finished telling her story to the young man and his wife, they were all on the verge of tears being overwhelmed with joy. A calmness filled the nurse as she became reflective, remembering listening to her son's heartbeat in the chest of her patent. As she hugged the young couple, the Spirit of God truly was in the room.

As we turn our attention to Jesus, we will realize that He is already looking out for us, even when we assume that He neither sees nor cares about what is happening in our lives. The Bible reminds us that the eyes of the Lord are on the righteous and His ears are attentive to their cry. Our Lord charges us to love Him with all our hearts and demonstrate our devotion to Him through a bond of unity with one another. Within that bond, the love will draw others to the love of Jesus Christ that is manifested in our lives. As we are brought to complete unity, the world sees that the Father sent Jesus and that He loves us even as He loves His Son.

Can God give life to those who are physically dead? Yes, God can do all things except fail. Jesus is greater than all the people, practices, and procedures of the Old Testament, and Apostle Paul, the author of the majority of the New Testament, explains how true that is. Jesus is the Son of God, the radiance of God's glory, and He represents the Father. Because of that, Jesus is greater than the angels and Moses. In fact, Jesus is God's ultimate apostle. He is our great high priest and an anchor for the soul.

Let us not fear anything, for God is with us. Do not be dismayed, for God is our Father. He will strengthen us and help us. He will uphold us with His righteous right hand. God's purpose applies to all people. Know and enjoy knowing God. He did not have to create humanity, but He did and know God is power. God has no needs, nor does He need us. He chose to create us so that we could fellowship with Him.

Let your light so shine in love.

Jesus loves us and died for us so that one day we may live with Him forever. Don't let go of the burden of faith in battles of spiritual warfare. Hold on to the burden of faith, even though it may cost your physical life. Martin Luther King Jr. saw a vision and continued to battle Satan, even in giving up his own life, and his vision is still pursued with intense enthusiasm today. We continue to overcome our racial divides, and one day a united people will be recognized throughout the world as God's people. John F. Kennedy showed no fear of Satan and his scheme to weaken the future of our country. This country is coming together to form a more perfect union of free immigrants, with people apprehending their inner natures and seeing progress intuitively.

The kingdom of heaven in the earthly realm is for all people, and the joy in life is the will of God. Our sinful natures began in the garden with Satan's war against humanity. Satan is determined to flourish against God, but as he was told in the garden, hope for mankind is coming. The Word of God (the Bible) incorporates, the Personality of God, the Son of God, and the Spirit of God,—all operating in the realms of heaven and earth to accomplish the Word of God. God rested on the seventh day because He was finished. All He had said and done was finished, and He will prevail for the earthly realm of heaven.

Sin has consequences. Mankind shall surely die in time and be resurrected in eternity. In time, mankind is purposed for God's plan, and life is a gift where death looms on two commandments of God:

(1) Thou shalt love the Lord thy God with all thy heart, and with all thy soul, and with all thy strength and with all thy mind

(2) And thy neighbour as thyself (Luke 10:27)

We do this, we shall live!

Remember yesterday, hope for tomorrow, but live for today. God has not changed from the beginning of creation, and He will not change today or tomorrow. God said, "I change not."

Amen.

Time
(Wikipedia, s.v. "Time,"
https://en.wikipedia.org/wiki/Time)

[1] B.V. Johnson, *High On the Mountain.* Quoted in D. C. Collier, *My Origin, My Destiny: Christianity's Basic "Value Proposition"* *(Bloomington, IN: Westbow, 2016): n.p.*

Alfred Lord Tennyson,
Former Poet Laureate of the United Kingdom
https://en.wikipedia.org/wiki/Alfred,_Lord_Tennyson

The Knowing Jesus Study Bible
The Holy Bible New International Version Copyright 1999
By the Zondervan (All Rights Reserved)

Printed in the United States
By Bookmasters